THE AUTHORESS
Salamah bint Saïd, afterward Emily Ruete

Memoirs of an Arabian Princess
of Oman and Zanzibar

The extraordinary life of a muslim princess
between East and West

by

Emily Said Ruete

TROTAMUNDAS PRESS

Trotamundas Press Ltd.
The Meridian, 4 Copthall House, Station Square, Coventry
CV1 2FL, UK

"Memoirs of an Arabian Princess " by Emily Said Ruete

published in 1907 by Doubleday, Page & Company,
New York

copyright © 2008 of this edition, Trotamundas Press Ltd.

ISBN: 978-1-906393-09-0

Trotamundas Press is an international publisher specializing in travel literature written by women travellers from different countries and cultures.

Our mission is to bring back into print great travel books written by women around the world which have been forgotten. We publish in several languages.

It is our privilege to rescue those travel stories which were widely acclaimed in the past and that are still relevant nowadays to help us understand better the diversity of the countries and the world.

The travel stories also make an enjoyable reading, full of adventure and the excitement of discovery.

We are proud to help preserving the memory of all those amazing women travellers which were unjustly forgotten and hope that you will enjoy reading about their interesting experiences as much as we have enjoyed researching them.

www.trotamundaspress.com

Emily Ruete a.k.a Sayyida bin Said,
Princess of Oman and Zanzibar
1844-1924

Emily Ruete was born Sayyida bin Said on August 30, 1844, the daughter of Sultan Said of Zanzibar and Jilfidan, a circassian concubine from his harem.

Her first years were spent in the Bet il Mtoni palace, by the sea outside Stone Town in the island of Zanzibar. She grew up bilingual in Arabic and Swahili and taught herself to write, a skill very unusual for women at the time, even for those from a royal household. In 1853 she moved with her mother to the palace of Bet il Tani. The Sultan, her father, died in 1856 when she was twelve years old and she inherited a plantation with a house and a large sum of money. Her brother Sayyid bin Said al-Said became Sultan of Muscat and Oman. Her other brother, Majid, became Sultan of Zanzibar.

Her mother died in 1859 and she inherited from her three plantations. The same year her two brothers Majid and Bargash were fighting for power. Sayyida favored Majid while her sister Khwala sided with Bargash.

She was only fifteen years old and she acted as secretary of Bargash party because she could write. The insurrection of Bargash against his brother Majid was brought to an end with the help of an English gunboat and Bargash was sent into exile in Bombay for three years. Sayyida retired to Kisunbani, one of her plantations.

Eventually she returned to Stone Town and Majid forgave her, a fact that earnt her the enmity of Bargash and Khwala. Other members of the family also rejected her and she turned her attentions to the europeans living in Zanzibar. One of these was Heinrich Ruete, who was working for a German trading company and who lived in the house next to Sayyida's.

They started a relationship and Sayyida became pregnant in 1866. Rather than facing the risk of being executed for having dishonoured her famiy, she escaped to Aden where she became a Christian, changed her name to Emily and married Heinrich Ruete. The baby, a boy, died a few months later but they eventually moved to Hamburg and had two daughters and one son: Antonia, Rosalie and Said.

In 1870, Heinrich Ruete died in a tram accident, leaving Emily with three small children and a difficult economic situation because the authorities denied her heritage claims.

She decided to write "Memoirs of an Arabian Princess" as a legacy for her children. The book was first published in the German Empire in 1996 and was later published in the United States and the United Kingdom.

The book is the first known autobiography of an Arab woman and presents a vivid picture of life in Zanzibar between 1850 and 1865 and an inside portrait of her brothers Majid and Bargash, the later Sultans of Zanzibar.

In 1888 Emily returned to Zanzibar with the intention of regaining back her cultural and financial inheritance but she was ignored by both the Arabs and the Europeans. After a few months in Zanzibar, she left for the Syrian coast where she lived for the following twenty five years. She eventually returned to Germany in 1914 and died of pneumonia in 1924.

There is nowadays a permanent exhibition about Emily Ruete in the People's Palace in Zanzibar, the palace that had been built by her brother, Sultan Bargash in Stone Town in Zanzibar.

PRINCE OTTO VON BISMARCK-SCHÖNHAUSEN

PREFACE

NINE years ago I conceived the idea of writing down some facts for the information of my children, who at that time knew nothing about my origin except that I was Arabian and had come from Zanzibar. Exhausted in body and in mind, I did not then expect to live until they were grown up, did not think I should ever relate to them verbally the happenings of my youth and the course of my fate. Hence I determined to record my story on paper. My memoirs were not at first intended for the general public, but for my children, to whom I wished to bequeath them as a heritage of faithful motherly love. Finally, however, upon urgent persuasion, I consented to have them published.

I finished these pages some years ago, and only the last chapter forms a recent addition, made because of a voyage I undertook to my old home, Zanzibar, with my children. May my book go out into the world, and may it meet with as many friends as was my happy lot to find.

Berlin, May, 1886.   EMILY RUETE,
née Princess of Oman and Zanzibar.

CONTENTS

xi

CONTENTS

ILLUSTRATIONS

CHAPTER I

Family History

IT WAS at Bet il Mtoni, our oldest palace in the island of Zanzibar, that I first saw the light of day, and I remained there until I reached my seventh year. Bet il Mtoni is charmingly situated on the seashore, at a distance of about five miles from the town of Zanzibar, in a grove of magnificent cocoanut palms, mango trees, and other tropical giants. My birthplace takes its name from the little stream Mtoni, which, running down a short way from the interior, forks out into several branches as it flows through the palace grounds, in whose immediate rear it empties into the beautiful sparkling sheet of water dividing Zanzibar from the continent of Africa.

A single, spacious courtyard is allotted to the whole body of buildings that compose the palace, and in consequence of the variety of these structures, probably put up by degrees as necessity demanded, the general effect was repellent rather than attractive. Most perplexing to the uninitiated were the innumerable passages and corridors. Countless, too, were the apartments of the palace; their exact disposition has escaped my memory, though I have a very distinct recollection of the bathing arrangements at Bet il Mtoni. A dozen basins lay all in a row at the extreme end of the courtyard, so that when it rained you could visit this favourite place of recuperation only with the help of an umbrella. The so-called "Persian" bath stood apart from the rest; it was really a Turkish bath, and there was no other in Zanzibar. Each bath-house contained two basins of about four yards by three, the water reaching to the breast of a grown-up person. This resort was highly popular with the residents of the palace, most of whom were in the habit of spending several hours a day there, saying their prayers, doing their work, reading, sleeping, or even eating and drinking. From four o'clock in the morning until twelve at night there was constant movement; the stream of people coming and leaving never ceased.

Entering one of the bath-houses—they were all built on the same plan—you beheld two raised platforms, one at the right and one at the left, laid with finely woven matting, for praying or simply resting on. Anything in the way of luxury, such as a carpet, was forbidden here. Whenever the Mahometan says his prayers he is supposed to put on a special garment, perfectly clean—white if possible—and used for no other purpose. Of course this rather exacting rule is obeyed only by the extremely pious. Narrow colonnades ran between the platforms and the basins, which were uncovered except for the blue vault of heaven. Arched stone bridges and steps led to other, entirely separate apartments. Each bath-house had its own public; for, be it known, a severe system of caste ruled at Bet il Mtoni, rigidly observed by high and low.

Orange trees, as tall as the biggest cherry trees here in Germany, bloomed in profusion all along the front of the bath-houses, and in their hospitable branches we frightened children found refuge many a time from our horribly strict school-mistress! Human beings and animals occupied the vast courtyard together quite amicably, without disturbing each other in the very least; gazelles, peacocks, flamingoes, guinea fowl, ducks, and geese strayed about at their pleasure, and were fed and petted by old and young. A great delight for us little ones was to gather up the eggs lying on the ground, especially the enormous ostrich eggs, and to convey them to the head-cook, who would reward us for our pains with choice sweetmeats.

Twice a day, early in the morning and again in the evening, we children—those of us who were over five years old—were given riding lessons by a eunuch in this courtyard, without at all disturbing the tranquillity of our animal friends. As soon as we had attained sufficient skill in the equestrian art, our father presented us with beasts of our own. A boy would be allowed to pick out a horse from the Sultan's stables, while the girls received handsome, white Muscat mules, richly caparisoned. Riding is a favourite amusement in a country where theatres and concerts are unknown, and frequently races were held out in the open, which but too often would end with an accident. On one occasion a race nearly cost me my life. In my great eagerness not to be outstripped by my brother Hamdan, I galloped madly onward without observing a huge bent palm tree before me; I did not become aware of the obstacle until I was just about to run my head against it, and, threw myself back, greatly terrified, in time to escape a catastrophe.

A peculiar feature of Bet il Mtoni were the multitudinous stairways, quite precipitous and with steps apparently calculated for Goliath. And even at that you went straight on, up and up, with never a landing and never a turn, so that there was scarcely any hope of reaching the top

THE SULTAN'S PALACE TO-DAY

Photograph by Coutinho Brothers, Zanzibar

unless you hoisted yourself there by the primitive balustrade. The stairways were used so much that the balustrades had to be constantly repaired, and I remember how frightened everybody was in our wing, one morning, to find how both rails had broken down during the night, and to this very day I am surprised that no accident occurred on those dreadful inclines, with so many people going up and down, the round of the clock.

Statistics being a science unfamiliar to the inhabitants of Zanzibar, no one knew exactly how many persons lived at the palace of Bet il Mtoni, but were I to hazard an estimate, I think I should not be exaggerating if I put the total population at a thousand. Nor will this large number seem excessive if one considers that whoever wants to be regarded as wealthy and important in the East must have an army of servants. No less populous, in fact, was my father's town palace, called Bet il Sahel, or Shore House. His habit was to spend three days a week there, and the other four at Bet il Mtoni, where resided his principal wife, once a distant relative.

My father, Seyyid Saïd, bore the double appellation of Sultan of Zanzibar and Imam of Muscat, that of Imam being a religious title and one originally borne by my great-grandfather Ahmed, a hereditary title, moreover, which every member of our family has a right to append to his signature.

As one of Seyyid Saïd's youngest children, I never knew him without his venerable white beard. Taller in stature than the average, his face expressed remarkable kindness and amiability though at the same time his appearance could not but command immediate respect. Despite his pleasure in war and conquest, he was a model for us all, whether as parent or ruler. His highest ideal was justice, and in a case of delinquency he would make no distinction between one of his own sons and an ordinary slave. Above all, he was humility itself before God the Almighty; unlike so many of great estate, arrogant pride was foreign to his nature, and more than once, when a common slave of long and faithful service took a wife, my father would have a horse saddled, and ride off alone to offer the newly wedded couple his good wishes in person.

My mother was a Circassian by birth, She, together with a brother and a sister, led a peaceful existence on my father's farm. Of a sudden, war broke out, the country was overrun by lawless hordes, and our little family took refuge "in a place that was under the ground"—as my mother put it, probably meaning a cellar, a thing unknown in Zanzibar. But the desperate ruffians found them out; they murdered both of my mother's parents, and carried away the three children on horseback. No tidings ever reached my mother as to the fate of either brother, or sister. She must have come into my father's possession at a tender age, as she lost her first tooth at his home, and was brought up with two of my sisters of her own years as companions. Like them she learned to read, an accomplishment which distinguished her above the other women in her position, who usually came when they were at least sixteen or eighteen, and by that time of course had no ambition to sit with little tots on a hard schoolroom mat. She was not good-looking, but was tall and well-built, and had black eyes; her hair also was black, and it reached down to her knees. Of a sweet, gentle disposition, nothing appealed to her more than to help someone who might be in trouble. She was always ready to visit, and even to nurse invalids; to this very day I remember how she would go from one sick bed to another, book in hand, to read out pious counsels of comfort.

My mother had considerable influence with Seyyid Saïd, who rarely denied her wishes, though they were for the most part put forward on behalf of others. Then, too, when she came to see him, he would rise, and step toward her—a signal distinction. Mild and quiet by nature, she was conspicuously modest, and was honest and open in all things. Her intellectual attainments were of no great account; on the other hand, she showed admirable skill at needlework. To me she was a tender, loving mother, which, however, did not prevent her from punishing me severely when I deserved it. Her friends at Bet il Mtoni were numerous, a rare circumstance for a woman belonging to an Arab household. No one's faith in God could have been stronger. I call to mind a fire, which broke out one moonlight night in the stables, while my father was in town with his retinue. Upon a false alarm that our house had caught, my mother seized me under one arm and her large Koran under the other, and ran out of doors. Nothing else concerned her, in that moment of peril.

So far as I can remember, my father—the Seyyid, or Sultan—had only one principal wife, from the time I was born; the other, secondary wives, numbering seventy-five at his death, he had bought from time to time. His principal wife, Azze bint Sef, of the royal house of Oman, held absolute sway in his home. Although small and insignificant-looking, she exercised a singular power over her husband, who fell in readily with all of her ideas. Toward the the Sultan's other wives and to his children she behaved with domineering haughtiness and censoriousness; luckily she had no children of her own, else their tyranny would certainly have been unendurable. Every one of my father's children—there were thirty-six when he died—was by a secondary wife, so that we were all equals, and no questions as to the colour of our blood needed to be raised.

This principal wife, who had to be addressed as "Highness" (for which the Arabic is Seyyid, and the Suahili Bibi), was hated and feared by young and old, high and low, and liked by none. To this day do I remember how stiffly she would pass everybody by, hardly ever dropping a smile or a word. How different was our kind old father! He always had a pleasant greeting to give, whether the person was one of consequence or a lowly subordinate. But my high and mighty stepmother knew how to keep herself on the top of her exalted rank, and no one ever ventured into her presence without being specially invited. I never observed her to go out unless grandly escorted, excepting when she went with the Sultan to their bath-house, intended for their exclusive use. Indoors, whoever met her was completely awestruck, as is a private soldier here in the presence of a general. Thus the importance she gave herself was felt plainly enough, although upon the whole it did not seriously spoil the charm of life at Bet il Mtoni. Custom demanded that all of my brothers and sisters should go and wish her a "good morning" every day; but we detested her so cordially that scarcely one of us ever went before breakfast, which was served in her apartments, and in this way she lost a lot of the deference she was so fond of exacting.

Of my senior brothers and sisters some were old enough to have been my grandparents, and one of my sisters had a son with a grey beard. In our home no preference was shown to the sons above the daughters, as seems to be imagined in Germany. I do not know of a single case in which a father or mother cared more for a son than for a daughter simply because he was a son. All that is quite a mistake. If the law allows the male offspring certain privileges and advantages—for example, in the matter of inheritance—no distinction is made in the home treatment given to children. It is natural enough, and human too, that sometimes one child should be preferred to another, whether here in this country or in that far southern land, even though the fact may not be openly acknowledged. So with my father; only it happened that his favourite children were not boys, but two of my sisters, Sharife and Chole. One day my lively young brother Hamdan —we were both about nine years old at the time —accidentally shot an arrow into my side, without, however, doing me much injury. The affair coming to my father's ears, he said to me: "Salamah, send Hamdan here"; and he scolded the offender in such terms as to make his ears tingle for many a day after.

The pleasantest spot at Bet il Mtoni was the *benjile*—close to the sea, in front of the main building—a huge, circular, open structure where a ball could have been given, had such a custom been in vogue with our people. This *benjile* somewhat resembled a merry-go-round, since the roof, too, was circular; the tent-shaped roof, the flooring, the balustrades, all were of painted wood. Here my dear father was wont to pace up and down by the hour with bent brow, sunk in deep reflection. He limped slightly; during a battle a ball had struck his thigh, where it was now permanently lodged, hindering his gait, and occasionally giving him pains. A great many cane chairs—several dozen, I am sure—stood about the *benjile*, but besides these, and an enormous telescope for general use, it contained nothing else. The view from our circular look-out was splendid. The Sultan was in the habit of taking coffee here two or three times a day with Azze bint Sef and all of his adult offspring. Whoever wanted to speak to my father in private would be apt to find him alone in this place at certain hours. Opposite the *benjile* the warship *Il Ramahni* lay at anchor the year round, her purpose being to wake us up early by a discharge of cannon during the month of fasting, and to man the rowboats we so often employed. A tall mast was planted before the *benjile*, intended for the hoisting of the signal flags which ordered the desired boats and sailors ashore.

As for our culinary department, Arabian cooking, and Persian and Turkish as well, prevailed both at Bet il Mtoni and Bet il Sahel. For both establishments harboured persons of various races,

with bewitching loveliness and the other extreme
fully represented. But only Arabian dress was
allowed to us, while the blacks wore the Suahili
costume. If a Circassian arrived in her flapping
garments or an Abyssinian in her fantastic draperies, either was obliged to change within three
days, and to wear the Arabian clothes provided
her. As in this country every woman of good
standing considers a hat and a pair of gloves
indispensable articles, in the East ornaments are
essential. In fact ornaments are so imperative
that one even sees beggar-women wearing them
while plying their trade.

At his Zanzibar residences and at his palace of
Muscat, in Oman, my father kept treasuries full of
Spanish gold coins, English guineas, and French
louis; but they contained as well all sorts of
jewellery and kindred female adornments, from
the simplest trifles to coronets set in diamonds, all
acquired with the object of being given away.
Whenever the family was increased, through the
purchase of another secondary wife or the birth
—a very frequent event—of a new prince or
princess, the door of the treasury was opened, so
that the newcomer might be suitably endowed
according to his, or her rank and position. In
case of a child being born, the Sultan would
usually visit mother and child on the seventh
day, when he would bring ornaments for the infant.
A newly arrived secondary wife would likewise

be presented with the proper jewellery soon after she was bought, and at the same time the head eunuch would appoint the domestics for her special service.

Although my father observed the greatest simplicity for himself, he was exacting toward the members of his household. None of us, from the oldest child to the youngest eunuch, might ever appear before him except in full dress. We small girls used to wear our hair braided in a lot of slender little plaits, as many as twenty of them, sometimes; the ends were tied together; and from the middle a massive gold ornament, often embellished with precious stones, hung down the back. Or a minute gold medal, with a pious inscription, was appended to each little plait, a much more becoming way of dressing the hair. At bed-time nothing was taken off us but these ornaments, which were restored next morning. Until we were old enough to go about veiled, we girls wore fringes, the same that are fashionable in Germany now. One morning I surreptitiously escaped without having my fringe dressed, and went to my father for the French bonbons he used to distribute among his children every morning, but instead of receiving the anticipated sweetmeats, I was packed out of the room because of my unfinished toilette, and marched off by an attendant to the place from which I had decamped. Thenceforth I took good care never to present myself incompletely beautified before the paternal eye!

Among my mother's intimates were two of the secondary wives who were Circassian, like herself, and who came from the same district as she did. Now, one of my Circassian stepmothers had two children, Chaduji and her younger brother Majid, and their mother had made an agreement with mine that whichever parent survived, should care for the children of both. However, when Chaduji and Majid lost their mother they were big enough to do without the help of mine. It was usual in our family for the boys to remain under maternal tutelage until they were about eighteen to twenty, and when a prince reached this age he was declared to have ccme to his majority, that is to say, the formalities took place sooner or later, according to his good or bad conduct. He was then considered an adult, a distinction as eagerly coveted in that country as anywhere else; and he was at the same time made the recipient of a house, servants, horses, and so on, beside a liberal monthly allowance.

So my brother Majid attained his majority, which he had merited rather by his disposition than his years. He was modesty itself, and won all hearts through his charming, lovable ways. Not a week passed but he rode out to Bet il Mtoni (for, like his deceased mother, he lived at Bet il Sahel), and although my senior by a dozen years played games with me as if we had both been of the same age.

Photograph by A. C. Gomes & Co., Zanzibar

RUINS OF PRINCESS SALAMAH'S EARLY HOME

One day, then, he arrived with the glad news that his majority had been announced by his father, who had granted him an independent position and a house of his own. And he besought my mother most urgently to come and live, with me, in his new quarters, Chaduji sending the same message. To his impetuous pleading my mother objected that without his father's consent she could not accept, and said she must therefore first consult him; as for her, she was willing enough to share Majid's and Chaduji's dwelling if they wished it. But Majid offered to save my mother this trouble by himself asking the Sultan's sanction, and the next day, in fact—my father happening to be at Bet il Sahel—he brought back the coveted permission. Thus our transmigration was decided upon. After a long talk between my mother and Majid, it was concluded that we should not move for a few days, when he and Chaduji would have had time to make the necessary arrangements for accommodating us.

CHAPTER II

Bet il Watoro

THE change, after all, was not an easy one for my mother. She felt deeply attached to Bet il Mtoni, since she had spent most of her life there; besides, she disliked novelty. Yet the idea of possibly being of some help to her friend's children outweighed her personal inclinations, as she afterward told me. Scarcely had her decision to move become known, when on all hands the complaint was addressed to her: " Jilfidan (this was my dear mother's name), is your heart closed to us, that you are deserting us forever?" "Ah, my friends," was her reply, "it is not by my will that I leave you; but my departure is ordained." No doubt some readers will mentally cast a glance of pity at me, or shrug their shoulders, because I say "ordained." Perhaps those individuals have hitherto kept their ears and eyes shut against the

will of God, rejecting His divine manifestations
while allowing mere chance full sway. It must,
of course, be noted that the author of this book
was originally a Mahometan, and that she was
brought up as such. Furthermore, I am telling
about Arabian life, about an Arabian household,
where—in a real Arabian family—two things
were totally unknown, that word "chance" and
also materialism. The Mahometan acknowledges
God not only as his creator and preserver; but
is conscious of the Lord's omnipresence, and
believes that not his own will, but the Lord's
must govern in all matters, great or small.

Several days sped by pending our preparations,
and we then waited for the return of Majid, who
was to supervise our journey in person. Three
playmates I particularly regretted leaving, two
of my sisters and one of my brothers, almost
exactly my age. On the other hand, I was overjoyed at the prospect of bidding adieu to our new,
unmercifully severe schoolmistress. Owing to the
forthcoming separation, our quarters resembled
a huge beehive. Everybody, according to their
circumstances and degree of affection, brought us
farewell presents—a very popular custom there.
However trifling the present he is able to give,
nothing will induce an Arab to withhold it from
the departing friend. I remember a case in point.
One day—I was quite a small girl then—after
visiting a plantation, we were about to start the

homeward journey to Bet il Mtoni in our boats. Suddenly, I felt a slight jerk at my sleeve, and upon turning round beheld a little old Negro woman. She handed me an article wrapped in banana leaves, saying: "This is for you, mistress, in honour of your departure; it is the first ripe thing from my plot." Speedily opening the leaves, I found a freshly picked head of maize. I did not know the old Negro woman, but subsequently learned that she was a long-standing favourite of my mother's.

Well, at last Majid arrived, with the announcement that the captain of the *Ramahni* had been ordered to send a cutter for us the next evening and another boat for the luggage and the escort. My father happened to be at Bet il Mtoni the day we were to leave, and we repaired to the *benjile* expecting to find him there. He was thoughtfully pacing up and down, when, seeing my mother approach, he came forward to meet her. They were soon absorbed in a lively conversation touching the journey, the Sultan having meanwhile commanded a eunuch to bring me some sweetmeats and sherbet, probably to stop my everlasting questions. As may easily be imagined, I was tremendously excited and curious regarding our future home, and in fact about everything that concerned the town-life. Up till then, I had been in town only once, and but for a very short time, hence I had the acquaintance of many brothers,

sisters, and stepmothers in store for me. We
eventually betook ourselves to the apartments of
the high and mighty Azze bint Sef, who graciously
vouchsafed to dispose of us standing up, a conces-
sion on her part, so to speak, because she usually
received and dismissed people in a sitting position.
My mother and I were privileged to touch her
dainty hand with our lips—and to turn our backs
upon the lady forever. Then we travelled up-
stairs and down, to say good-bye to our friends,
but barely half were in, so my mother determined
to go back at the next hour for prayer, when she
would be sure to see them all.

At seven in the evening our large cutter—not
used except on special occasions—appeared before
the *benjile*. She was manned by a dozen sailors,
I remember, and at the stern, as well as at the
bow hung a plain crimson flag, our ensign, which
bears no pattern nor any kind of symbol. The
rear part of the vessel was covered with an expan-
sive awning, and under this were silken cushions
for perhaps ten persons. Old Johar, a trusted
eunuch of my father, came to inform us that
everything was in readiness; he and another
eunuch had been ordered to accompany us by the
Sultan, who watched us from the *benjile*. Our
friends saw us to the door with weeping eyes, and
their sorrowful "Wedah! Wedah!" (Good-bye!
Good-bye!) rings in my ears to this very day.

Our beach was rather shallow, and we had no

landing stage of any sort.   There were three methods, however, of reaching your boat.   You sat
on a chair, which was transported by lusty sailor-
men; or you mounted on one of their backs; or
you simply walked across by a plank from the
dry sand to the edge of the craft, and this was the
method chosen by my mother, only she was supported on either side by a wading eunuch.   Another eunuch carried me over, and put me down
in the stern with my mother and old Johar.
The cutter was lit with coloured lamps, and as
soon as we started the rowers intoned a slow
rhythmic chant, according to Arabian custom.
We skirted the coast-line, as usual, while I went
fast asleep.   I was awakened by the sound of
many voices calling out my name.   Decidedly
startled, though half drowsy, I observed that we
were arriving at our destination.   The boat
stopped almost under the windows of Bet il Sahel;
they were brilliantly illuminated, and full of spectators, mostly my strange brothers and sisters and
stepmothers.   Some of the children were younger
than myself, and no less anxious to make my
acquaintance than I theirs; it was they who
clamoured for me so loudly when the expected
cutter appeared.   The landing was accomplished
in the same manner as the embarkation.   My
young brothers greeted me with more than enthusiasm, insisting, too, that we must accompany
them at once; but my mother of course declined,

SEA FRONT OF THE CITY OF ZANZIBAR

Photograph by A. C. Gomes & Co., Zanzibar

since otherwise Chaduji, who was then already waiting at the window of her own house, would have been disappointed by the delay. To be sure I was grieved enough at not being allowed to go with my brothers and sisters immediately, having long looked forward to that happy moment, yet I knew my mother well enough to be aware that she would not change her mind once it was made up; despite her incomparably unselfish love toward me, she was always quite firm and resolute. Meanwhile she comforted me by promising to take me to Bet il Sahel for a whole day upon my father's return thither.

So we passed on to Bet il Watoro, Majid's house, which lay quite close to Bet il Sahel, and likewise commanded a fine view of the sea. We found my sister Chaduji awaiting us at the foot of the stairs. She welcomed us right heartily to Bet il Watoro, and led us to her apartments, where a servant soon brought us all kinds of refreshments. Majid and his friends remained in the anteroom, not being allowed to come up until Chaduji sent permission by my mother's request. And how delighted that splendid, noble Majid was at being able to welcome us to his home!

Our own room was of fair size, and from it was visible a neighbouring mosque. It was furnished like most Arabian rooms, and we found nothing lacking. One room was sufficient for us; wearing the same sort of clothes by night as by day, people of rank, with their fastidious cleanliness, can easily dispense with special rooms set apart for sleeping. Persons of wealth and distinction arrange their dwellings about as follows:

Persian carpets or daintily woven, soft mats cover the floor. The thick whitewashed walls are divided into compartments running perpendicularly from floor to ceiling, and these niches contain tiers of wooden shelves painted green, forming a succession of brackets. On the brackets stand arrayed the most exquisite and costly articles of glass and china, in symmetrical order. An Arab does not care what he spends in adorning his niches; let a handsomely painted plate or a tasteful vase or a delicately cut glass cost what it may, if it looks well he buys it. An effort is made to hide the bare spaces of wall between the compartments. Tall mirrors are put there, reaching from the low divan to the ceiling; they are usually ordered from Europe, with the dimensions exactly specified. Mahometans disapprove of pictures as trying to imitate the Divine creation, but latterly this objection has been losing force to some extent. Clocks, on the other hand, are in great vogue, and in a single house one often sees a whole collection; some are placed at the top of the mirrors and some in pairs on either side.

In the gentlemen's rooms the walls are decorated with trophies of valuable weapons from Arabia, Persia, and Turkey, with which every

Arab embellishes his abode in the measure of his
rank and riches. A large double bed of rosewood,
adorned with marvellous carvings of East Indian
workmanship, stands in the corner, shrouded
entirely with white tulle or muslin. Arabian beds
have very long legs; to get in the more com-
fortably you mount on a chair first, or borrow the
hand of a chambermaid for a step. The space
under the bed is often utilised for sleeping pur-
poses too, for instance by nurses of children or
invalids. Tables are quite rare, and only found
in the possession of the highest personages, though
chairs are common, both in kind and quantity.
Wardrobes, cupboards, and the like are unfamiliar furniture, but you find a sort of chest with two
or three drawers and a secret place besides for
money and jewellery. These coffers—several of
them to each room—are large and massive, and
studded with hundreds of small brass-headed nails
by way of ornaments. Windows and doors we
would leave open all day, never shutting the windows at all except for a little while when it rained.
Hence, the phrase "I feel a draught" is unknown
in that country.

At first my new quarters did not suit me in the
least; I missed my young brothers and sisters
too much, and Bet il Watoro seemed so cramped
and confining when I thought of the immense
Bet il Mtoni. "Am I to live here forever?" I
continually kept asking myself the first few days;

"and am I to sail my boats in a washtub?" for
there was no river Mtoni here, so that the water
had to be fetched from a well outside the house.
When my good, kind mother, who would have
liked to give away everything she owned, advised
me to present my nice sail-boats, that I was so
fond of, to my brothers and sisters at Bet il Mtoni,
I would not hear of it. In short, I experienced
feelings I had never undergone before, of great
unhappiness, and I was deeply afflicted. But my
mother was in her element. With Chaduji, she
was occupied all day in planning and settling household affairs, so that I saw very little of her.
Majid gave me the most attention; the day after
my arrival he took me by the hand, and showed
me his whole domicile, from top to bottom. Only
I could see nothing to admire; in fact I begged
my mother fervently to go back with me as soon
as possible to Bet il Mtoni and my accustomed
playmates. This was of course out of the question,
especially as she was genuinely useful in her new
sphere.

I was glad to find a lover of animals in Majid,
who kept a great variety of them. His white
rabbits caused my mother and Chaduji fearful
annoyance, since they ruined the new house.
He also had a number of fighting cocks, from
every corner of the earth; such a rich collection
I have never even seen in a zoölogical garden.
So I got into the habit of accompanying Majid

whenever he visited his pets, and he most good-naturedly allowed me to share in his amusements. No very long period elapsed before I became the possessor—through his kindness—of a veritable army of fighting cocks which rendered my solitary existence at Bet il Watoro a great deal easier to bear. Nearly every day we marshalled our champions, conducted before us and taken away again by slaves. A cock-fight is by no means a dull business; the spectator's attention is fully engrossed, and the whole thing offers an entertaining, sometimes a comical, performance.

Later on Majid taught me how to fence with sword, dagger, and lance, and when we went into the country together we would practise pistol and rifle shooting. Thus I developed into something like an Amazon, to the utter dismay of my mother, who entirely disapproved of fencing and shooting. But I very much preferred manipulating these weapons to sitting still by the hour over needle or bobbin. Indeed, my new pursuits coupled with complete freedom—another mistress had not been found for me yet—soon cheered my spirits, so that my former aversion to the solitary Bet il Watoro began to fade. Nor did I neglect horsemanship; Mesrur, a eunuch, was ordered by Majid to continue the instruction he had begun. As I have said, my mother had little time to devote to me privately, being so monopolised by Chaduji. The result was that I attached myself by degrees to a trustworthy Abyssinian; her name was Nuren, and I learned some Abyssinian from her, though I have forgotten it all long ago.

We remained in constant communication with Bet il Mtoni, where our friends received us with the warmest hospitality. Otherwise we kept in contact through verbal messages delivered by slaves. People do not care to correspond in the East, even if they know how to write. Everyone there of wealth and station owns several slaves, good runners particularly reserved for the transmission of messages. A runner must be able to cover a lot of ground in a day, but he is unusually well-treated and cared for; on his discretion and integrity—since he is intrusted with the most confidential matters—the welfare, or more, of his owners may depend. Occasionally a messenger of this kind for the sake of revenge destroys life-long relations of friendship. However, that induces few individuals to learn writing, and thus make themselves independent of their slaves for life; nowhere is the term "easy-going" fraught with deeper significance than in our country.

My sister Chaduji was extremely fond of company; hence Bet il Watoro often resembled nothing so much as a dove-cote. Hardly a day in the week but the house would be full of visitors from six in the morning till twelve at night. The guests arriving at six of the forenoon and intend-

PANORAMA OF THE CITY OF ZANZIBAR

Photograph by Coutinho Brothers, Zanzibar

ing to stay all day were met by the servants, and shown to a special apartment, waiting there until eight or nine before they were received by the mistress of the house. The interval between their arrival and formal reception, those lady visitors would spend in making up the lost hours of sleep in the aforesaid room.

Though a close affection existed between myself and Majid, I was unable to conceive the same sort of liking for Chaduji. Imperious and fault-finding, her character differed in great degree from her brother's; and in this view of their unlikeness I was not alone, as everyone acquainted with both was well aware which was the more affable of the two. She was wont to be very cool, and even offensive, toward strangers, thereby gaining enemies rather than friends. Anything new or foreign inspired her with strong repulsion; despite her renowned hospitality, she was much put out if a European lady sent in her name, although such a call would last only a half or three-quarters of an hour at the very most. I confess she was a good, intelligent housekeeper, scarcely knowing a moment's idleness, and if any spare time did fall to her she would go sewing and stitching away as busily at clothes for her slaves' younger children as at other times she would be working at my brother Majid's shirts. I remember that three of these children were delightful little boys, whose father performed the functions of an architect in our service. They were my juniors by a few years, but as I lacked companions of my own age they became my regular playmates, until I finally grew acquainted with my other brothers and sisters at Bet il Sahel.

CHAPTER III

Bet il Sahel

A CROSS-GRAINED DOORKEEPER—FASCINATIONS OF
CHOLE—THE VERANDA AT BET IL SAHEL—
LIFE IN THE COURTYARD—AN OUTDOOR BUTCH-
ERY, KITCHEN, AND LARDER—LOVE OF ARABS
FOR THEIR HORSES—SOCIAL DISTINCTIONS AT
TABLE—WHY BET IL SAHEL WAS PREFERABLE
TO BET IL MTONI—RACE HATRED BETWEEN
CIRCASSIANS AND ABYSSINIANS—CURSHIT—
ENFORCED TUITION

THE day I had so ardently longed for at last
arrived—that day, the whole of which I was to
spend at Bet il Sahel, whither my mother and
Chaduji were to take me. It was on a Friday—
the Mahometan Sunday—that we left our house
quite early in the morning, probably at five or six
o'clock. We had not far to go, however, as our
destination was scarcely more than a hundred
steps away.

The faithful, but unbearably cantankerous old
doorkeeper gave us anything but an amiable
welcome. He complained that he had been on his
shaky old pins for the last hour answering female
visitors. A Nubian slave belonging to my father,
his beard had grown white in honourable ser-

vice; I say "beard" advisedly, because male Arabs are in the habit of shaving their heads. My father was much attached to him, particularly since this servant had once saved him from committing a hasty act which he might have regretted all his life, by knocking a sword out of his hand just as he was about to strike down a man who had roused his anger. But we small children had no respect for the old fellow's virtues, and in the exuberance of a frolicsome mood would often play naughty tricks on this ancient and worthy servitor. We were particularly fond of abstracting his keys, and I suppose there was hardly a room in the whole of Bet il Sahel where they had not lain hidden from him at one time or another. One of my young brothers seemed to have a peculiar aptitude for secreting those keys in places unsuspected even by us conspirators.

Ascending from the ground floor to the first story, we found the ladies of the house all astir and active, only that the exceptionally pious were still engaged in their morning devotions, and hence invisible to the outer world, No one would think of disturbing a Mahometan at prayer under any circumstances, no, not even if the house should take fire. Our father was one of the devout worshippers on this occasion, and so we were obliged to wait until his prayers were done. Our visit had purposely been arranged to coincide with his presence at Bet il Sahel, to which, in

fact, the unusual concourse was due. It must
not be imagined that the ladies assembled were
all friends or acquaintances of ours. On the contrary, some were entire strangers to us, and most
of these came from Oman, our virtual mother-
country, to ask my father for assistance of a
material kind, which, indeed, was rarely denied.
Our mother-country is as poor as our relatives
there, and our own prosperity really dated from
my father's conquest of the rich island of Zanzibar.

If the law prohibits, in general, a woman from
holding personal intercourse of any sort with a
strange man, it makes two exceptions, in favour
of the sovereign and of the judge. Now, as thousands and thousands are totally ignorant of
penmanship, and therefore cannot make their
petitions in writing, nothing remains for such
needy ones but to come themselves, even if they
have to undertake the little journey from Asia to
Africa. At all events, my father used to endow
his petitioners according to their rank and position,
omitting to harass the poor wretches with a lot
of questions, as the custom is in Europe. It
was assumed that nobody would go begging other
people's help for pure amusement's sake, and I
daresay this may frequently apply to Germany
as well.

My brothers and sisters—whether previously
acquainted with me or not—were all most cordial
in their manner of welcome, none more so than

the perfect Chole, dear to my memory forever. Hitherto the affections of my young heart had been entirely devoted to my sweet mother, but now I began to worship this angel of light as well. Chole soon became my ideal; she was greatly admired by others and was Seyyid Saïd's favourite daughter. Anyone judging her impartially and unenviously felt obliged to acknowledge her extraordinary beauty; and where is the human being completely insensible to the charm of beauty? Bet il Sahel contained no such misanthropist, at any rate. This sister of mine was without peer in our family, her good looks being positively proverbial. Though fine eyes are not at all uncommon in the East—as everyone must be aware —she was invariably called Star of the Morning. An Arab chief from Oman once inflicted an injury upon himself through falling too deeply under the spell of her fascination. In the course of a sham fight, enacted before our house, the chief caught sight of her at a window, and became so enraptured with Chole's appearance that he forgot everybody and everything about him, and in this fit of amorous abstraction planted the point of his spear into his foot, not noticing the blood and feeling no pain, until awakened from his blissful dream by one of my brothers.

Bet il Sahel is relatively much smaller than Bet il Mtoni, and is likewise situated hard by the sea; there is something smiling and pleasant about the place which is reflected in the residents. All the living-rooms of Bet il Sahel command a glorious view of the water and the shipping. Well do I remember the enchanting scene. The doors of the living-rooms—which are all on the upper story—open on a long, broad veranda, the most magnificent I have ever seen. The veranda has a roof supported by pillars reaching to the ground, and has a balustrade along its entire length. Numerous chairs were set out, and coloured lamps hung up, which by night lent the house an aspect of fairyland. You looked down over the balustrade into the courtyard—the liveliest, noisiest spot imaginable—communication between which and the upper story being maintained by means of two large stairways. It was up and down, down and up, all day and all night, and often there was such a crowd at the foot or head of the stairs that it was difficult to reach them.

In a corner of the yard cattle were slaughtered, skinned, and cleaned in quantities, all for the sole use of the house, which, like every house in Zanzibar, must provide its own meat. In another corner sat Negroes having their heads shaved, while near them a lot of lazy water-carriers lay full length on the ground, paying not the slightest attention to the urgent calls for water, until unpleasantly reminded of their duty by a muscular eunuch. I have known these leisurely gentlemen to start up, and to dash away like lightning with their jugs at the mere frown of their formidable taskmasters. Near by nurses sunned themselves and their little charges, whom they were regaling with fairy tales and stories. The kitchen, too, was in the open, and the smoke ascended freely to heaven as it might fancy, for chimneys do not exist. Strife and confusion were the rule among the host of culinary sprites, the head cooks dealing out boxes on the ears in liberal style to the quarrelsome or dilatory scullions of either sex. In the Bet il Sahel kitchen the animals were cooked whole, and I have seen a fish arrive carried by two sturdy blacks; small fish were not taken in excepting by the basketload, nor fowl but by the dozen. Flour, rice, and sugar were reckoned wholesale by bags, while the butter, imported from the north, especially from the island of Socotra, came in jars of a hundredweight each. Only spices were measured by the pound. Still more astonishing was the quantity of fruit consumed. Every day thirty or forty, or even fifty, men brought loads of fruit on their backs, apart from the consignments delivered by the little rowboats which supplied the plantations along the shore. I am probably making no extravagant estimate if I put Bet il Sahel's daily consumption of fruit as high as the capacity of a railway van; but some days, for instance, during the mango harvest, the demand would be still larger. The slaves intrusted with all this fruit were extremely care-

BRINGING FRUIT INTO TOWN

less; they would plump the heavy baskets from their heads violently to the ground, so that half the contents would be bruised or squashed.

The place was protected against the sea by a long wall about twelve feet thick, and when the tide was low some of the horses were tethered in front of this wall so that they might roll in the sand and enjoy themselves. My father was immensely attached to his thoroughbred steeds from Oman; he saw them regularly, and if one fell sick he would go to the stable, and satisfy himself that it was properly attended to. The fondness of Arabs for their favourite horses I can prove by my brother Majid's example. He owned a very handsome brown mare, and was exceedingly anxious that she should have a colt. So, when the time came for the fulfilment of this hope, he gave orders that he should be notified of the birth at whatever hour it might occur. Thus, we were actually roused up out of bed one night, at about two o'clock, to be informed of the happy event. The groom who bore the welcome news received a fine present from his overjoyed master. But this is no exceptional case; in Arabia Proper the devotion to horses is said to be still more intense.

Between half past nine and ten my elder brothers left their apartments to take breakfast with my father, in which repast not a single secondary wife, however great a favourite with the

Sultan, was allowed to share.   Besides his children and grandchildren—those who had passed infancy, that is to say—the only persons admitted to his table were the principal wife Azze bint Sef and his sister Assha. Social distinctions in the East are never observed more rigorously than at meals; one is extremely cordial and affable toward one's guests, just as people of high station are here in Europe, or perhaps even more so, though at meals one excludes them from one's company.   The custom is so ancient that no one takes offence.   In Zanzibar the secondary wives had a system of sub-distinctions.   The handsome and expensive Circassians, fully conscious of their superior merits and value, refused to sit at table with the brown Abyssinian women.   Thus each race, in accordance with a tacit understanding, kept to itself when eating.

At Bet il Sahel I got the impression that the residents of the place were a much gayer set than at Bet il Mtoni.   The reason was that at Bet il Mtoni, Azze bint Sef ruled supreme over husband, stepchildren, their mothers, in short over everybody, whereas at Bet il Sahel, where Azze rarely appeared, everyone, my father not excepted, felt free and untrammelled.   And I think my father must actually have appreciated this liberty of action very keenly, as he had for years sent no one to Bet il Mtoni for permanent residence unless by such person's request, although that place alway had rooms empty, and the other was crowded. The overpopulation I speak of at last gave rise to so much inconvenience that my father hit upon the idea of putting wooden pavilions on the broad veranda to serve as living rooms; eventually he had another house built—which went by the name of Bet il Ras (Cape House)—on the sea-coast a few miles north of Bet il Mtoni, and which was designed particularly for the younger Bet il Sahel generation.

A painter would have found rich material for his brush on the veranda at Bet il Sahel. To begin with, there were quite eight or nine different facial hues to be taken account of, and the many colours and shades of the garments worn would have offered the most vivid contrasts. No less lively was the bustle and stir. Children of all ages tore about, squabbled, and fought; shouting and clapping of hands—taking the place of the Western bell-ringing—for servants, resounded incessantly; the enormous, thick, wooden sandals of the women, sometimes inlaid with silver or gold, made a distressing clatter. We children enjoyed the confusion of tongues immensely. Arabic was supposed to be the only language spoken, and in the Sultan's presence the rule was invariably obeyed; but no sooner was his back turned than a sort of Babel would break loose, Persian, Turkish, Circassian, Suahili, Nubian, Abyssinian, to say nothing of dialects. However,

no one took exception to mere tumult but now
and then an invalid, and our dear father was
quite used to it, and never objected in the least.

Here, then, on the veranda, my sisters were
assembled the day of my visit. They were festally
clad in celebration of our Sunday and of Seyyid
Saïd's coming; the mothers walked up and down
or stood in groups, talking and laughing and
joking so vivaciously that one not knowing the
country would never have taken them for the
wives of the same man. From the stairs sounded
the clinking of arms worn by my brothers, who
had also come to see their father, in fact, to spend
the whole day with him.

More luxury and extravagance prevailed than
at Bet il Mtoni, and I found better looking women
than there, where my mother was the only Circassian but one. Here, on the other hand, the
majority of the Sultan's wives were Circassians,
who undoubtedly are much finer in appearance
than the Abyssinians, though among them, too,
great beauties may be seen. Of course these
natural advantages gave rise to envy and malice
on the other side: a Circassian of noble bearing
would be avoided, if not detested—having offended
no one but the chocolate-coloured Abyssinians simply because she looked dignified. Under such circumstances it was natural enough if ridiculous
race hatreds manifested themselves among the
children. Her virtues notwithstanding, the Abys-

sinian is usually of a spiteful, revengeful disposition, and when she flies into a temper goes beyond the limits not only of moderation but of decency. We daughters of Circassian mothers were called "cats" by our sisters who had Abyssinian blood in their veins, because some of us had the misfortune to possess blue eyes. And then they spoke to us sarcastically as "your Highness," as further proof of their indignation at our having come into the world with white skin. Nor did they forgive my father for selecting as pets his two daughters Sharife and Chole from the loathsome tribe of cats.

Under the oppressive Azze bint Sef, life at Bet il Mtoni had always been more or less cloistral; at Bet il Watoro I felt still lonelier; consequently I relished the cheerfulness and the movement at Bet il Sahel all the more. Two little nieces of mine, daughters of my brother Khaled, were brought from their home every morning to Bet il Sahel—and taken back in the evening—so that they might do their lessons with their young uncles and aunts, and play with them afterward. Curshit, Khaled's mother, a Circassian by birth, was a very unusual woman. Of heroic bodily stature, she combined extraordinary will power with a highly developed intelligence, and I do not remember encountering her equal among the members of my sex. On one occasion that Khaled represented my father, during his absence, it was said she governed our country, with Khaled as her puppet. Certainly her counsel was invaluable to our family, and her decisions were momentous. Her two eyes were so sharp and observing that they saw as much as Argus's hundred eyes. In matters of importance she showed the wisdom of Solomon. But the small children found her repulsive, and gladly avoided her.

Evening came at last, and we began to think of returning to Bet il Watoro. Suddenly my father announced, to my mother's infinite dismay, that I must resume my lessons. Upon her plea that it had been impossible to find a suitable governess, he decreed that I was to be sent to Bet il Sahel each morning, and taken back in the evening, like my two nieces; thus I should be instructed together with my brothers and sisters there. To me this news was most unpleasant: I was far too wild to get any joy out of sitting still; besides, my last mistress had altogether spoilt my taste for lessons. Yet momentarily the prospect of being with my brothers and sisters all day—except on Fridays—comforted me, especially as my charming sister Chole offered to take charge of me and watch over me. And so she did—like a mother. My real mother grieved terribly over my father's order separating us six days in a week, but of course, she was obliged to acquiesce. She however bade me show myself several times during the day at a certain spot, by which means she could catch a glimpse of me from Bet il Watoro, and wave her greetings.

CHAPTER IV

FURTHER REMINISCENCES OF CHILDHOOD

JUVENILE TRICKS—PRINCESS SALAMAH CLIMBS A
PALM TREE—MAJID'S SEIZURE—A FAMILY QUAR-
REL WHICH ENDS IN DIVORCE AND AN-
OTHER CHANGE OF ABODE FOR THE AUTHORESS
—EXTRAVAGANCE OF A PERSIAN SULTANA—
MORE DIVORCE—LESSONS IN CALIGRAPHY

I LIKED Bet il Sahel more and more, for we
had our own way there to a far greater extent
than at Bet il Watoro. Nor did we miss many
opportunities to play silly tricks, and when
punishment was the result I fared better than
the others, on account of Chole's extreme good
nature.

We owned several handsome peacocks, one of
which possessed an ugly disposition and could
not endure us children. One day, as five of us
were crossing over from Bet il Sahel to Bet il
Tani—a sort of annex to the former—the peacock
in question suddenly made a furious attack upon
my brother Djemshid. We all immediately
pounced upon the monster and vanquished it,
but were much too angry to think of letting it go
without a reminder for its misconduct. So we
concluded upon a hideous revenge, and pulled out

the bird's handsomest tail feathers. And what a
pitiful wreck that proud, bellicose beauty looked
then! Luckily our father happened to be in Bet il
Mtoni that day, and the affair was hushed up by
the time he returned.

I remember that two Circassians joined us, from
Egypt, and that we children noticed how haughty
one of them was, ignoring us completely, in fact.
This struck at our vanity; we accordingly tried
to hatch out some scheme for the offender's un-
doing. It was no easy matter to reach her, as
she avoided us, and we never had any dealings
with her. But this only aggravated us the more,
especially as she was our senior by only a few years.
One day, passing her room, we found the door open.
She was sitting on a fragile Suahili bed, constructed
of little else but a mat attached by cords to four
posts. She was merrily singing some national
ditty to herself. My sister Shewane acted as
ringleader; she gave us a significant glance of
which we, all kindred spirits, were not slow to
catch the meaning. In a moment we had rushed
in, seized the bed at its four corners, lifted it up
as high as we were able, and let it bump down to
the floor again, to the great terror of the amazed
occupant. It was a childish trick, but was war-
ranted by the effect it had, which was to cure our
victim of her indifference toward us for good and
all, so that ever after she was affability itself.
Our object was therefore attained.

But occasionally I would play some prank on my own account. Once, soon after our removal to Bel il Watoro, I risked my neck in a humorous adventure of the sort. One morning I made my escape, and climbed a tall cocoanut palm as quick as a cat and unaided by a *pingu*, the stout rope that even expert climbers never dream of dispensing with. Having got half-way up, I impudently began to call down my greetings to the passers-by. What a fright they got into! A group of alarmed individuals collected round the tree, imploring me to come down with all the caution I could muster. It was out of the question to send anyone up for me; in climbing a palm tree, one's hands are fully occupied, and one cannot take care of a child besides oneself. However, I was enjoying myself capitally, and not until my mother appealed to me in heart-broken accents of despair, promising me all sorts of fine things, would I vouchsafe to descend, which finally I did, sliding down with great deliberation, and reaching the ground in safety. That day I was everybody's pet; presents were showered upon me to celebrate my fortunate deliverance from danger, though I really deserved a severe flogging. We were always playing some trick or other, no punishment deterring us from the continuation of our naughtiness. There were seven of us, three boys and four girls, who kept the house lively, and often, alas, got our poor mothers into trouble.

Now and then my dear mother kept me at home on some other day than Friday, which opportunities the indulgent Majid seized upon to spoil me thoroughly. It was on one of those occasions that he gave us a terrible fright. He was subject to frequent cramps, whence he was rarely, if ever, left unattended, Even if he took a bath, my mother and Chaduji, whose confidence in the servants was limited, took it in turn to watch at the door, exchanging a few words with him from time to time, when he would indulge in his favourite pleasantry of exclaiming "I am still alive!" Thus Chaduji, while walking to and fro outside the bathroom door one day, suddenly heard a heavy thud inside. Entering, in great perturbation, she found my beloved brother on the floor, in the throes of a violent attack—the worst he had ever suffered. A mounted messenger was at once despatched to Bet il Mtoni, to summon my father.

From their ignorance about diseases in general, the people of Zanzibar are dupes of quackery; indeed, now that I am familiar with the natural and rational treatment of diseases by competent doctors, I feel tempted to believe that many deaths at home must have been due to barbarous medical methods rather than to sickness.

Unfortified with that adamantine faith in our "destiny," I hardly know how we should have supported our grief over the numerous deaths among our family and retainers. Poor Majid, who lay unconscious for hours in his spasms, was obliged to breathe air which would have been injurious to the healthiest person. Despite our great indoor love of free, fresh air, an invalid, especially if suspected of visitation by the Evil One, is rigidly secluded from the outer atmosphere, and his room, as well as the whole house, vigorously fumigated.

The Sultan landed about an hour after Majid's seizure in a *mtumbi*, a tiny fishing boat holding only one person. He hastened to the house, and though the parent of more than forty children was passionately affected by the illness of one. Bitter tears coursed down his cheeks as he stood at the sick bed, crying out' aloud "Oh, Allah, oh, Allah, preserve my son!" Thus did he pray without ceasing. The Most High listened to his petition, and Majid was restored to us.

When my mother questioned the Sultan as to his reason for coming in such a miserable craft, he replied: "At the moment the messenger arrived, there was not a boat of any kind ready on the shore, and none could have been obtained without first being signalled for. I had no time to spare, and did not even want to wait for a horse to be saddled. Just then I happened to catch sight of a fisherman in his *mtumbi* close to the *benjile;* I hailed him, caught up my arms, jumped in, and made off immediately." Now you must know that a *mtumbi* is nothing but the trunk of a tree hollowed out, is supposed to hold but one, and is propelled by a double paddle instead of oars. Narrow, short, and pointed at the bow, it therefore differs from what is known in Germany as the "Greenland canoe." In this country too it must sound strange that a man plunged into anxiety about his son's life should yet think of his weapons. Well, customs vary all the world over. As to the European the Arab's fondness for his arms is incomprehensible, so the Arab mind has much difficulty in understanding some of the Northern usages. Just now the awful toping by the male sex occurs to me as an example.

Thus I went to school every day at Bet il Sahel, returning each evening to my mother at Bet il Watoro. After having learnt about a third of the Koran by heart, I was supposed to have done with school, at the age of nine. Thenceforth I repaired but on Fridays to Bet il Sahel—my father's day there—in the company of my mother and Chaduji.

We went on living contentedly in this way at Bet il Watoro for two years. But good times cannot be expected to last; usually some unforeseen and untoward event disturbs one's peace. So in our case.

The cause of strife in our household was a creature than whom none could have been more

charming and lovable. Assha, a distant relative
of ours, had recently come from Oman to Zanzibar,
where she was soon taken to wife by Majid. We
were all devoted to her, and all rejoiced over
Majid's happiness, with the single exception of
his sister Chaduji, who, I deeply regret to confess
wronged Assha entirely, from beginning to end.
Assha, I have remarked, was in every respect
charming; besides, she was quite young, so
that Chaduji ought to have instructed her, and
by degrees have imparted dignity to her. But
she treated her with scorn and enmity. Her
marriage to Majid entitled Assha to first place in
the household; nevertheless, Chaduji patronised
her so that the poor, gentle soul would go weeping to my mother, to complain of this unwarranted
treatment. My mother's situation between two
fires, as it were, became most difficult and un-
enviable. Chaduji declined to surrender any of
her imaginary rights, and continued to look upon
Assha as an irresponsible child. In vain did my
mother endeavour to rectify her views, and to
make her recognise the position of Majid's wife;
in vain she besought her to spare Majid whatever
annoyance she could, for his own sake. Yet it
was all done in vain. Our once agreeable existence
at Bet il Watoro became unbearable, and in order
to escape from a scene of perpetual discussion my
mother decided to leave the house she liked so well.

Majid and his wife would not hear of her departure, Assha being quite inconsolable; Chaduji, on the other hand, remained unmoved, which served to strengthen my mother in her resolve. Assha herself at last felt she could put up with Chaduji's autocratic ways no longer, and obtained a divorce from Majid. The poor thing took her wretched experiences in Zanzibar so to heart that she would none of the country or its inhabitants. Under favour of the south wind she sailed back to Oman, where she had an aunt living in the neighbourhood of Muscat, the capital, both her parents having died. As for my mother and me, our removal had been planned for some time, and we migrated to Bet il Tani. My sister Chole was delighted, as we now were almost under her very roof; she in fact secured and arranged our new quarters for us.

The Sultan's houses were all so crowded that it was no easy matter to get rooms, and gradually a habit had arisen of counting upon vacancies through death. It was really abominable to see a woman prick up her ears at another woman's cough, as if hoping for a case of consumption. Sinful as such thoughts must appear, they were of course due to this overcrowding. My mother and I owed it to Chole that we got a fine, large room at Bet il Tani without having to wait for somebody's decease. Chaduji we rarely saw now; she felt insulted by our change of abode, and accused my mother of lack of affection for her,

Photograph by Mr. Samuel Zwemer

TYPE OF OMAN ARAB

quite wrongfully, to be sure. But my mother
had simply been unable to endure Chaduji's
oppression of the girl whose chief offence was
having become Majid's wife. He continued to
visit us, however, and to remain one of our best
friends.

Bet il Tani was situated in immediate proximity
to Bet il Sahel, and was connected with it by a
bridget hat passed over a Turkish bath-house
midway between the two. At the time I speak
of Bet il Tani presented but a shadow of its former
splendours. On its first story there had once
lived a Persian princess, Shesadeh by name.
She was one of my father's principal wives and a
great beauty. Said to have been enormously
extravagant, she nevertheless had the reputation
of great kindness toward her stepchildren. A
hundred and fifty Persian horsemen, who occupied
the ground floor, formed her modest suite; she
rode and hunted with them in the open light of
day, which, according to Arabian notions, was
going rather too far. The Persian women seem
to receive a sort of Spartan education; they have
a great deal more liberty than ours, but are coarser
both in thought and behaviour.

Shesadeh, I was told, had led a most luxurious
life. Her clothes—Persian style—were literally
stitched with genuine pearls from top to bottom;
if a servant, sweeping the rooms, found any on
the floor, the princess would always refuse to take

them back. She not only made desperate inroads upon the Sultan's bounty, but transgressed against sacred laws. Marrying my father for his wealth, her heart was bestowed on another. The Sultan went nigh to incurring blood-guiltiness one day, in the heat of his anger, when a faithful attendant stayed his arm, saving Shesadeh from death and my father from a dreadful sin. Nothing but divorce was possible after that; fortunately the union had been childless. Some years later the Sultan was fighting the Persians at Bender Abbas, on the Persian Gulf, when, it was reported, the handsome Shesadeh was observed with the hostile forces, aiming at members of our family.

In that princess's erstwhile home I began to learn writing on my own account, and after a very primitive method. Of course this had to be done in secret, as women are never taught to write, and any knowledge they may acquire of it must not be discovered. For a first lesson I took the Koran, and tried to imitate the characters on the shoulderblade of a camel, which in Zanzibar does duty for a slate. Success inspired me with encouragement—I made quick progress. But eventually I needed some guidance in caligraphy proper, so I imposed upon one of our "educated' slaves the huge honour of acting as my writing master. Somehow the affair came to light, and torrents of obloquy descended upon me. But not a rap cared I!

CHAPTER V

National Singularities

THE VAUNTED ACTIVITY OF NORTHERN PEOPLES—
INFANT DRESS—A CLIMATE FAVOURING EASE
—PRAYER FIVE TIMES A DAY—INTERVENING
PURSUITS—CHEWING BETEL—GOING TO BED
—MENU À LA ZANZIBAR—REAL COFFEE

OVER and over again I have been asked: "How on earth do the people manage to exist in your country, without anything to do?" And the question is justifiable enough from the point of view of the Northerner, who simply cannot imagine life without work, and who is convinced the Oriental never stirs her little finger, but dreams away most of her time in the seclusion of the harem. Of course, natural conditions vary throughout the world, and it is they that govern our ideas, our habits, and our customs. In the North one is compelled to exert oneself in order to live at all, and very hard too, if one wishes to enjoy life, but the Southern races are greatly favoured. I repeat the word "favoured" because the frugality of a people is an inestimable blessing; the Arabs, who are often described in books as exceedingly idle, are remarkably frugal, more so perhaps than any but the Chinese. Nature her-

self has ordained that the Southerner can work,
while the Northerner must.   The Northern nations
seem to be very conceited, and look down with
pride and contempt upon the people of the tropics
—not a laudable state of mind.   At the same time
they are blind to the fact, in Europe, that their
activity is absolutely compulsory to prevent them
from perishing by the hundred thousand.   The
European is obliged to work—that is all; hence
he has no right to make such a great virtue of
sheer necessity.   Are not Italians, Spaniards, and
Portuguese less industrious than Germans and
Englishmen?   And what may the reason be?
Merely that the former have more summer than
winter, and consequently that they have less of a
struggle for existence.   A cold climate implies
the providing and securing oneself against all
sorts of contingencies and actualities quite unknown in southern lands.

Luxury plays the same part everywhere.   Who
has the money and the inclination will find opportunity to gratify his fancies, whatever quarter
of the globe he may inhabit.   So let us leave
this subject untouched, and confine ourselves
to the real necessities of life.   If in this country
the new-born infant requires a quantity of things
to protect its frail existence against the perversi-
ties of a changeable climate, the little brown-
skinned Southerner lies almost naked, slumbering
easily while fanned by a perpetual current of

warm air. If in Germany a two-year-old child needs shoes, stockings, pantalettes, a couple of petticoats, a dress, an overcoat, gloves, scarf, gaiters, muff, and a fur cap, whether it belongs to a banker or a labourer—the quality being all that differs—in Zanzibar the costume of a royal prince of the same age comprises two articles, shirt and cap. Then why should an Arabian mother, whose demands for herself and child are so small, work as hard as a German housewife? She has never heard of darning gloves and stockings, of performing the sundry labours done for a European child once a week.

A certain great institution of European households we are ignorant of—washday. In Zanzibar we wash every day whatever needs washing, and in half an hour's time the things are all dry, pressed (not ironed), and put away. We also dispense with curtains, which besides being troublesome and keeping out the sunlight, have to be kept clean and in repair. An Oriental woman, whatever her rank, tears her clothes to a surprisingly limited extent, which is natural enough, since she does not move about so much, frequents the public thoroughfares less, and possesses fewer garments.

All these, and several other considerations help to make the Oriental woman's lot more bearable and comfortable than the European's, without particular regard to social station. But

in order to be familiar with the details of their
daily life one must have spent some time among
them.   Tourists, who make only a brief sojourn
in those parts, and who, perhaps, get their information from waiters at hotels, are scarcely to be
considered as credible witnesses.   European ladies
who may actually have penetrated into a harem,
perhaps in Constantinople or in Cairo, are still
unacquainted with the real harem; they have
only known its outer semblance in the rooms kept
for show, rooms where European finery is partially
aped.   Besides, the climate is so generous and
beneficent that one hardly need trouble about
the morrow.   I do not deny that the people down
there are disposed to taking things easy, but
remembering the heat of July and August in
Europe, one may conceive what sort of effect the
tropical sun would have upon one.

The Arab has no leaning toward commerce and
industry; he cares for little else than warfare and
agriculture.   Few Arabs take to a special trade
or profession; they make indifferent merchants,
though much given to bartering; the Semitic
sense of business they appear to lack.   His frugality enables the Arab to make ends meet easily,
and as a rule he thinks only of the immediate
present.   He never plans for the distant future,
for he knows that any day may be his last.   Thus
the life of the Oriental glides smoothly and easily
along.   Still, I now am describing only the life

in Zanzibar and Oman, which in various respects
differ from other Eastern countries.

The Mahometan's day is regulated—if that is
not saying too much—by his religious devotions.
Five times a day does he bend the knee to God,
and if he properly performs all the contingent
ablutions and changes of raiment in accordance
with scriptural ruling, fully three hours will be
consumed. The rich are awakened between four
and half-past five for the first prayer, after which
they return to bed, but the common people begin
the day's work with their first prayer. In our
establishment, where hundreds of inmates tried
to follow their individual tastes, it was hard to
maintain fixed rules, although the two general
repasts and the devotions compelled a measure
of systematic order. Most of us, then, slept on
again until eight o'clock, when the women and
children were roused by a gentle and agreeable
kneading process, at the hands of a female servant.
A bath of fresh spring water was ready, and likewise our wearing apparel, strewn the night before
with jessamine or orange blossoms, and now
scented with amber and musk. Nowhere in the
world is the cold bath used and appreciated more
than in the East. After dressing, which usually
took up an hour, we all went to see our father,
to wish him "good morning," and then to partake
of the first meal. To this we were summoned
by a drum, but as the table was completely set

beforehand, much less time was occupied in eating than the European method demands.

It was then that the day's real activities opened. The gentlemen prepared for the audience chamber, while the ladies—who were not obliged to work— took seats at their windows, to watch the passing in the street below, and to catch such private glances as might occasionally be thrown up at them. This provided great amusement; only sometimes a cautious mother or aunt would contrive to coax one away from the coign of vantage. Two or three hours thus sped quickly by. Visits were meanwhile being exchanged among the gentlemen, the ladies sending out servants with verbal appointments for the evening. Sedately minded persons, however, went to their airy apartments, where, either alone, or in small groups, they did needlework, stitching their veils, shirts, or trousers with gold braid, or a husband's, son's, or brother's shirt with red or white silk, which needed particular skill. The remainder would read stories, visit sick or well friends in their rooms, or attend to other private affairs. By this time it was one o'clock. Servants came to remind us of the second prayer. The sun was at its height then, so that everyone was glad to open the early part of the afternoon reposing, in a thin, cool garment, on a soft, prettily woven mat with sacred inscriptions worked upon it. Between dozing, chatting, and nibbling at fruit or cake, the time passed very pleasantly until four o'clock, when we prayed for the third time; a more elaborate toilette followed, and we repaired again to the presence of the Sultan, to wish him "good afternoon." The grown-up children were allowed to call him "father," but the little ones and their mothers had to address him as "Sir."

Now came the second and last meal of the day, at which the family would assemble. Upon its termination, the eunuchs would carry European chairs out upon the broad veranda, but only for the adults; the small people stood up as a mark of respect for age, which is held in greater reverence there than anywhere else. The family gathered about the Sultan, while a row of smart, well-armed eunuchs lined the background. Coffee was passed round, as well as beverages prepared from the essence of French fruits. The conversation was accompanied by a stupendous barrel organ, the biggest I ever saw; by way of change one of the large music boxes would be set going, or a blind Arabian girl named Amra, who was gifted with a lovely voice, would be ordered to sing.

In about an hour and a half the family separated, each following his or her own devices. Chewing *betel* was a favourite pastime. It is a Suahili habit, so that the Arabs of Arabia Proper find no pleasure therein; but those of us born on the east coast of Africa, and brought up among

Negroes and mulattoes, took to the habit quite readily, in spite of derision from our Asiatic relatives. We chewed *betel* surreptitiously, however, while absent from the Sultan, who had forbidden the practice.

With the aid of miscellaneous diversions the brief space slipped by till sundown, announced by musketry fire and drumming on the part of the Indian guard. This also constituted a signal for prayer. But the fourth observance was the most hurried of the day, since everybody not intending to pay visits would be expecting guests at home—sisters, stepmothers, stepchildren, secondary wives. For entertainment there was coffee and lemonade, cakes and fruit, jesting and laughing, reading aloud, playing cards (but not for money or any other stake), singing, listening to the *sese* being played upon by a Negro, sewing, stitching, lace-making—just as one felt inclined.

So it is altogether wrong to suppose that the rich Oriental woman has nothing to do. True, she neither paints, plays the piano, nor dances (as understood here). But those are not the only existing methods of passing the time. Down there we are all contented; to us the feverish, everlasting chase after new pleasures and enjoyments is quite foreign. From the European point of view, therefore, the Oriental might no doubt be looked upon as a Philistine.

Upon retiring for the night we dismissed the

Photograph by Mrs. Emma Shaw Colcleugh

NATIVE MUSICIAN

male servants, who joined their families, living in separate dwellings apart from the house. The oil lamps were usually left burning, the candles only being extinguished. The custom of sending children over two years to bed at a certain hour had died out; they chose their own time, and often their own place, for going to sleep, so that occasionally they would have to be picked up tenderly by slaves, and transported with the least possible noise to their own little cots. Whoever had neither gone out, nor had received visitors, generally retired at ten o'clock, though some preferred to enjoy the air on the flat, well-swept roof until midnight. At about half-past seven the fifth and last prayer was supposed to be offered up. But just then one is likely to have company, or be otherwise engaged; hence a rule permitting postponement of the final devotions till bedtime. Women of wealth go to sleep by the assistance of two female slaves; one repeats the kneading operation, the other manipulates a fan. To wash the feet first in *eau de Cologne* is most refreshing. I may have mentioned that women keep all their clothes on, including their jewellery.

Returning to the culinary department, I must give some details about the eating arrangements in my father's palace at Zanzibar. We had no special dining room, but took our meals on the veranda. There the eunuchs spread along *sefra* with all the food for the whole repast. A *sefra* somewhat resembles a billiard table in shape; it is only a few inches high, however, and around the top runs a wide ledge. Although we possessed a lot of European furniture—lounges, tables chairs, and even a few wardrobes—we nevertheless sat down to eat in true Oriental fashion, upon carpets or mats next to the floor. Precedence by rank was strictly observed, the Sultan taking the head; near him were the senior children, the little ones (those over seven) coming at the end.

We had numerous dishes, often as many as fifteen. Rice formed a staple at each meal, and various preparations of it were in vogue. In the way of meat, mutton and chicken were preferred. We also ate fish, oriental breads and sundry pastry and sweetmeats. Contrary to the German system, all the food was placed on the table before anybody sat down. This obviated the need of service, and the eunuchs would step back, lining up at a little distance, ready to answer commands. Frequently the Sultan would send one of them, with a particularly savoury morsel, to a child not old enough to eat at the table, or perhaps to an invalid. I remember the special corner at Bet il Mtoni where I used to receive the platefuls he consigned to me. We mites got the same food as the grown-up people, but of course it was a privilege to have it selected by our father, who himself derived great pleasure from this.

Upon sitting down, everyone said grace in a

Photograph by A. C. Gomes & Co., Zanzibar

NATIVE COFFEE-PEDDLER

low but distinct tone: "In the name of Allah the all merciful." After eating the formula was: "Thanks be to the Lord of the Universe." Our father was always first to take his seat, and first to rise. One plate to each individual was not the custom, all the dishes (except the rice) being served in a number of little plates standing symmetrically along the *sefra*, so that a couple would eat from the same plate. There was no drinking simultaneous with the eating, but afterward sherbet or sugared water was obtainable. Nor was conversation usual, excepting when the Sultan spoke to someone; the rest of the time silence prevailed—a good thing, too. Fruit or flowers were never to be seen on the *sefra*. A few minutes before and after the meal slaves offered basins and towels, in order that one might wash one's hands. We chiefly used our fingers when we ate solids, which came upon the table cut up into small pieces. For spoons we had employment, but knives and forks were not brought out unless to honour European guests. Persons of refinement scented their hands, besides washing them, to drive away the odour of food.

Half an hour after the repast eunuchs handed round genuine Mocha in tiny cups resting on gold or silver saucers. In the East the coffee is thick and syrupy, but filtered clear; invariably drunk without milk or sugar, it is taken without any sort of eatables, though sometimes delicate slices of areca nut are provided. The coffee is poured out immediately prior to consumption, which task requires such skill that only few servants are fitted for it. The coffee-bearer carries the handsome pot, made of tin adorned with brass, in his left hand, while in his right he holds only a single small cup and saucer. Behind or next to him an assistant carries a tray with empty cups and a large reserve pot of coffee. If the company has dispersed, these men have to follow the various members, and insure their partaking of the delicious beverage. How highly coffee is esteemed by the Orientals, everybody knows. The greatest care being bestowed upon its preparation, it is specially roasted, ground, and boiled whenever wanted, and therefore is always taken perfectly fresh. Roasted beans are never kept, nor boiled coffee, either, when in the least degree stale, being then thrown away or given to the lower servants.

Our second and last general meal was at four in the afternoon, and since it corresponded exactly to the first I shall not describe it. We indulged in nothing else but light refreshments, such as pastry, fruit, or lemonade.

CHAPTER VI

CEREMONIES FOR THE NEWLY BORN

BIRTH—TIGHT BANDAGING—SHAVING OF THE HEAD
—PROTECTION AGAINST THE EVIL-EYE—THE
SITTING CEREMONY—BLACK NURSES AND EURO-
PEAN—HARDINESS OF ORIENTAL CHILDREN

THE birth of a prince or a princess, though not
greeted with salvoes of artillery, was nevertheless
always a happy event, in spite of jealousies to
which it might give rise. Seyyid Saïd and the
mother would not be alone in their gladness; we
little ones honestly participated in their joy because the ceremonies for infants newly come into
the world were numerous, and the festal doings
involved our small presences. There were usually
five or six accessions a year to our family.

The professional *accoucheur* is unknown among
Mahometans, who only engage midwives, these
however being incredibly ignorant. They generally came to Zanzibar from India, being preferred
to the natives, but why I have never succeeded
in finding out, since the Indian midwives are just
as devoid of practical knowledge as the Arabian
or Suahili. Certain it is that if mother and child
manage to survive, they have God and their own

constitutions to thank, and not those stupid creatures. After I was grown up some of my married friends told me about the primitive methods which the ignorant bunglers employed, and which would hardly bear public repetition.

When the child has been thoroughly washed in warm water, its neck and armpits are sprinkled with scented powder, and it is put into a little calico or muslin shirt. It is then laid on its back, the arms and legs are straightened out, and the whole body is tightly wound in a bandage from heel to shoulder, the extremities being covered thus as well as the trunk. Forty days and nights does the infant remain imprisoned, and is only released for bathing, which happens twice a day. The object of this bandaging is to give the child a good, erect carriage. The baby is watched by its mother with loving care, however many servants she may have at her disposal. Slaves alternate in rocking the spacious, handsomely carved wooden cradle, which, according to season, is protected by mosquito netting. But rarely does the mother rock the baby, and when she makes this exception, she regards it as a sort of amusement. If the new arrival be a girl, the ears are pierced with a needle on the seventh day after her birth. Six holes are usually made in both ears, which upon the lapse of a few weeks are loaded with heavy rings forever. I say forever, because she who wears none is either in mourning, or else has no holes in her ears.

When it is forty days old a peculiar ceremony is performed upon the child, which would be almost impossible in Europe—namely, the shaving of the head. How surprised my German nurse was in Hamburg at my infant daughter's long black hair, and how great was her impatience until my husband purchased a brush. The shaving of the head is done by the chief eunuch amid special formalities, from which fumigation with a kind of india-rubber must never be omitted. And the first hairs taken off are considered as a great treasure; they may neither be burnt, nor thrown on the dust heap, but they are buried in the ground, cast into the sea, or hidden in the crack of a wall. Twenty or thirty people witness the shaving, and the chief eunuch, whose experience as barber is limited to such occasions, runs no small risk of damaging the precious skull. Our "court tonsorialist" and his assistant would always be liberally rewarded by my father.

On this same auspicious day the baby is disencumbered of the aforesaid bandage. It is dressed up in a silk shirt, and a cap with gold braid, earrings, anklets, and bracelets. At this date, too ceases the careful seclusion of the child from the outer world, as up till now none but the parents, a few privileged friends, and the servants have been allowed to see it. For the rule of privacy the popular belief in the evil eye and all kinds of sinister spells is responsible.

Undoubtedly Oriental children look much prettier at this time of their life than European, because these wear too much white. Though I have been in Germany for years, I cannot change my opinion; in fact my own children looked dreadful to me in their baby clothes. The contrast with my beautifully apparelled nephews and nieces was most unfavourable. Perfumes were freely employed in Zanzibar. The child's bedding, towels, and all its garments were first scented with sweet jessamine, and again with amber and musk just before use, and finally sprinkled with attar of roses. Only it should be borne in mind that doors and windows were constantly open nearly the whole year round, which counteracted whatever noxious effects this singular custom might otherwise have entailed.

For a child's protection against the supposed evil-eye it is given certain amulets, which with the lower classes consist of an onion, a piece of garlic, a bone, or a shell perhaps, fastened to the left arm in a small leather bag. Instead of amulets, the higher classes take sayings from the Koran engraved on gold or silver medals, suspended from the neck by a chain. Boys keep these medals up to a certain age only, but girls often continue wearing them, though they also affect the so-called "guardian." This is a tiny book, of two inches by one and a half, reposing in a gold or silver case, and also hung from the neck by a chain.

Besides the mother's milk the baby soon receives other milk, several times a day, boiled with ground rice and sugar, and poured into a cup bearing a long spout. The bottle was quite unknown in my day, and infants got no other food until their teeth came, when they could eat anything they liked. They were not carried about much, but preferably set down on a carpet, where they could roll and tumble to their hearts' content.

As soon as a child makes its first attempts at sitting, another ceremony is enacted. Mother, nurses, and child wear their finest raiment. The child is placed on a square, medium-sized cart, which has very low wheels, and is cushioned with pillows and draperies. A short, slender pole stands up vertically at the end of the axle nearest the cart, and a little leg is put on each side of the pole. Meanwhile some Indian corn has been roasted by a peculiar process, so that the grains have swelled up to the size of thimbles; they are mixed with a lot of silver coins, and the whole conglomeration is then scattered over the child's head, young brothers and sisters making a tremendous rush for the spoils.

Until their feet are strong enough to bear sandals—wooden for females, and leather for males—children simply go barefoot. Neither sex ever wears stockings at any age, but a lady of rank is apt to do so when she rides on horseback, since custom demands concealment of the ankles.

At the age of three or four months, to the child's nurses are added a couple of slaves, who remain its property from that date. The older it grows, the more slaves it becomes entitled to, and if one dies the father bestows another or a corresponding sum of money. Every prince stays altogether with the women of the household until his seventh birthday, when he is circumcised in consonance with the Mosaic rite. Performed in the father's presence, this ceremonial involves lavish hospitalities stretching over three days. At this time, too, the boy is given a horse for his own, so that he learns the equestrian art early, in fact he acquires the sort of proficiency and agility one would only expect of a circus rider. We were innocent of proper saddles and of stirrups, at home, and therefore a firm seat was something to boast of.

Our nurses, even if they had served but a very short while, were highly considered, and greatly respected all their lives. Their original condition was that of slavery, but as a rule they were given their freedom in recognition of fidelity and devotion. The most anxious mother can safely leave her offspring to its nurse, who is likely to regard the son or daughter as a real parent might, and to treat it accordingly. What a contrast to the neglect and the heartlessness of German nurses! Many a time, out walking, have I felt inclined to scold one of those menials, though she might be a stranger to me, for cruelty to her tender charge. How different the behaviour of a black nurse! To begin with, she may have been in the service of her mistress for years, may actually have been born in her house. Hence she is, of course, unlikely to have many private interests, and is so unhindered from making those of the family her own. And then the very important circumstance that a black nurse very frequently, indeed generally, need not separate from her own child, which receives the same nourishment as the mistress's, the same brew of milk, the same chicken. It is bathed with its more exalted comrade, whose cast-off clothes it inherits. Its mother's occupation as a nurse ended, it still remains the other child's playmate, and none but an evil soul would be guilty of misconduct toward a foster-brother or sister.

This somewhat patriarchal system may account for our nurses being so much more devoted and trustworthy than the European, whom I have often pitied, in spite of their odious deficiencies, because they were obliged to leave their little ones for the sake of money. I have been told that those women do not feel the pang as keenly as I imagine, but I cannot believe it. Our native nurses are however conspicuous for one bad quality; they tell their young charges the most incredible, monstrous stories and legends, either to entertain or to quiet them. Lions, leopards, elephants, and witches figure the most prominently in these hair-raising recitals, which are sometimes enough to terrify adults. Nor does any amount of remonstrance seem to change the habit.

Upon the whole, it is much easier to bring up children in the South than in the North; they are spared the eternal colds, which lead to so many other things. But they are self-reliant and active, their luxurious life notwithstanding, and have greater opportunity to scamper about and play out of doors. Formal gymnastics do not exist; on the other hand, a boy's taking a run and leaping over a horse, or even two horses, excites no surprise. High jumping is a favourite sport at which everyone tries to outdo everybody else. Swimming forms an equally popular diversion, and is invariably self-taught, while the pursuit of shooting is taken up with enthusiasm quite early. Although boys go armed to the teeth, and carry as much powder and shot as men, one rarely hears of an accident happening through carelessness.

Only to a certain age does the young prince dwell under the paternal roof; after that a separate residence is assigned him, where he sets up independently—with his mother, if she happens to be living. The Sultan would pay him a monthly sum by way of allowance, which might be raised at his marriage, upon an increase of his family, or in case of irreproachable conduct, but not otherwise. If war broke out in Oman—a regrettably frequent occurrence—all the princes, including those half-grown, were obliged to join the forces and take part in the fighting like the common soldiers. The discipline at home was strict, but it tended to heighten the respect of the Sultan's sons for their father, and to make them honour him the more. As a little tot I often noticed how one of my elder brothers, anticipating a servant, would offer my father his sandals, that had been deposited by their owner at the door at entering the room.

There is scarcely anything to say about the rearing of the princesses; they are brought up at first in the same way as the boys, only that after the seventh year the male children have far more liberty outside the house. However, the juvenile princess has a broad, heavy silver comb put in her hair, following the local fashion, so that the back of her head may be flat when she is grown up. Should she marry one of her cousins—more plentiful in Oman than in Zanzibar—she naturally quits her father's roof, exchanging it for her husband's. Keeping unwed, she has the choice between continuance under her father's care and the protection of a brother. Each sister has a pet brother, and vice versa; in joy and in sorrow do they cling affectionately together, comforting and supporting one another at all times. Laudable enough in itself, to be sure, this sentiment yet stirred up jealousy and quarrels, and all sorts of family strife.

Upon occasion a sister would plead the Sultan's pardon for a delinquency committed by her favourite brother.　To his daughters he was always willing to turn an indulgent ear, especially the elder ones.　Did any of these come before him, he would advance to meet them, and would allow them to sit beside him on the sofa, while the grown up sons and we small people stood by in proper awe and humility.

CHAPTER VII

School

SCHOOL is of small importance to the Oriental. In Europe the life of Church and State is bound up with that of the schools, influencing all, from prince to pauper. Here the individual depends very largely, both as regards the development of his character and the hopefulness of his future prospects, upon his scholastic career, which has so little significance in the East, and which to many dwellers of those parts has no existence. Let me begin my disquisition on this subject by describing the system in vogue at my home.

At the age of six or seven all my brothers and sisters, without exception, were supposed to commence their schooling. We girls needed only to learn reading, but the boys had to learn writing as well. For the conduct of instruction there was one female teacher at Bet il Mtoni and one at Bet il Sahel, either having come from Oman upon my father's behest. When therefore the mistress

75

fell sick, and was confined to bed, we rejoiced greatly over the obligatory holiday, since no substitute could be obtained. We had no special schoolroom. The lessons took place on an open veranda, to which pigeons, parrots, peacocks, and bobolinks enjoyed unrestricted access. This veranda overlooked a courtyard, so that we could amuse ourselves by watching the lively proceedings down below. Our academical furniture consisted of one enormous mat, and equal simplicity distinguished our apparatus for study: Koran with its stand, a small pot of ink (domestic manufacture), a bamboo pen, and a well-bleached camel's shoulderblade. Easy to write upon with ink, this last-named serves as a slate; one's nerves are spared the screeching of the slate pencil. The camel bones were usually cleaned off by slaves. Our first task was to acquire the complicated Arabic alphabet, which done we began to practice reading in the Koran, our only text-book, the boys, as I have already mentioned, receiving tuition in writing besides. When some progress had been attained in reading we did it all together in chorus, at the top of our voices. And that was all, for no explanations are ever given. Hence but one in a thousand understands properly, and can interpret, the thoughts and precepts which the Mahometan scriptures embody. To analyse holy writ shows impiety; it is strictly forbidden, and one is expected to believe what one is taught.

By seven o'clock in the morning, after partaking of some fruit, we were on the veranda, awaiting the mistress. Pending her arrival, we would have jumping and wrestling matches, and would clamber about the balustrade, doing our best to risk our lives. One of us would be stationed as sentinel at a suitable place, whence a fictitious cough warned us of the pedagogic approach. In a twinkling every pupil was down on the mat, looking the picture of innocence, and upon her actual appearance we all bounded to our feet, to pay the tyrant obsequious reverence. In one hand she bore a huge metal ink pot, and in the other the odious bamboo cane. So we stood up deferentially until she had seated herself, when we followed her example. We all sat, cross-legged, surrounding the teacher. First she recited the opening chapter, or *sura*, of the Koran, which runs thus: "In the name of the most merciful God. Praise be to God, the Lord of all creatures, the most merciful, the King of the day of judgment. Thee do we worship, and of Thee do we beg assistance. Direct us in the right way, in the way of those to whom Thou hast been gracious, not of those against whom Thou art incensed, nor those who go astray." Then we jointly repeated this *sura* after her, concluding with the usual amen. Hereupon the lesson of the preceding day was reviewed, upon which new tasks in reading or writing were begun. Instruction continued until nine, being resumed from after breakfast to the second hour of prayer, about one o'clock.

Everyone was permitted to bring a few slaves to school; they took position somewhere in the background, while we children arranged ourselves on the mat as we pleased. Neither regular seats nor division into classes were customary; still less was there any attempt at the term reports that cause such tremendous excitement here. If a pupil was particularly backward or exceptionally forward, if remarkably good conduct or the reverse had been observed, the mother and the Sultan would be notified verbally. Rigid orders had been given by our father that we were to be thoroughly punished for such delinquencies as we might commit. Viewing our unruly conduct, the mistress had frequent occasion to swing that detested stick.

Besides reading and writing a little ciphering was taught; mental arithmetic involved numbers up to one hundred, while on paper one thousand was the limit. Anything beyond these figures was regarded as pernicious. Not much pains are bestowed on grammar and orthography. As for history, geography, physics and mathematics, I never heard of them at home, and not until I came here did I get acquaintance with these branches of study. But whether I am really any better off for my small amount of learning, which I laboriously obtained here by dint of untiring industry, than my friends in Africa, still remains an open question to me. I can say with full veracity, though, that I was never so egregiously hum-bugged and brow-beaten as after acquiring the most valuable treasures of European knowledge. Oh, you happy souls over there, you cannot even dream of what may be done in the exalted name of civilisation!

Of course the whole plan of our schooling for-bade anything like preparation after hours. How-ever much the mistress may be feared, she is highly respected by her pupils, who all their lives treat her with consideration and esteem. She indeed is occasionally called upon to act as media-tor between persons unable to agree on some point, thus fulfilling an office here entrusted by Catholics to their spiritual shepherd. But one thing Orien-tal scholars have in common with Western. I mean the natural instinct to bribe their teachers with presents. When my children in Germany begged me for a trifle to buy flowers for Miss So-and-So, I could not help recalling my own youth. This trait is not peculiar to any one nation, but may be found all the world over. Before I ever knew there was such a place as Germany I used to offer my instructress—as the rest did too—numerous sweetmeats, in order to curry favour with her; the most delicious French bonbons our father gave us would we attempt to sacrifice upon the altar of propitiation. Unfortunately, the object of our assiduities was a victim to toothache, and therefore rather cold toward our diplomacy, her idea being that by feeding her on sweets we hoped to make her toothache so bad that she would be obliged to give us a holiday.

The length of the course was quite uncertain. Whatever was to be learnt had to be learnt, and it depended on your own abilities whether you finished in one, two, or three years. Needlework formed no part of the curriculum, but was left to the mothers, who were usually expert in its practice. Still, I have known some of my sisters to grow up unable to sew on a button. Public schools exist too, though only for poor people's children. Everyone who can afford it keeps a governess or tutor. Sometimes the teaching devolves upon the secretary to the head of the family, but of course he would have charge of the girls only while they were extremely young.

It is inevitable that, having been brought up where I was, I should make comparisons with the European system, of which my children enjoyed the privileges. There certainly is a great disparity between German over-education and Arabian ignorance; too much is exacted on the one side, too little demanded on the other. But I suppose such sharp differences will never cease, but will persist to the end of the world, as no race appears capable of settling upon a golden mean. Here, at all events, the children have their minds stuffed with a great deal more than they can possibly absorb. Their schooldays once begun, the parents see very little of them. Owing to the sundry tasks that have to be prepared for next day, true family life is out of the question, and with this loss a steady, telling influence upon the juvenile character must in many cases be forfeited. All day long it is not living, but hurry and scramble, scramble and hurry, from one lesson to another. What a lot of time they waste, too, in arduously gaining facts destined to prove utterly useless, inasmuch as they seem to be imparted for the sole purpose of being forgotten! How approve a method by which the young are robbed of time that were much better spent at home?

Besides, the poor things are confined every day for five or more hours in a prison-like space called "schoolroom," hot and stuffy beyond description. Four tumblers to drink water out of allowed by an institution harbouring two hundred children! Would this not disgust a mother who wanted to kiss her child upon its return from that place? And why express surprise if under such conditions the little ones fall ill? Do for them what one may at home to keep them in health, the foul air of the schoolhouse must frustrate all one's efforts. How wretched many of the scholars look in this country, and how your heart bleeds for their deplorable state! Give me that open, airy veranda of ours. What profits the highest education so the body be ruined in the struggle to possess it?

I notice little here of that respect which we all,
my brothers, sisters, and self, accorded to our
parents and teachers, in fact, to age generally.
Neither does the religious instruction given at the
schools seem to be as effective as it ought, and
no wonder, since it takes a purely mechanical form;
endless lists of dates pertaining to ecclesiastical
history are the children compelled to learn by
heart, instead of being urged to observe a regular
attendance at church, where a good sermon would
inspire them far more than those barren historical
facts. We had to memorise lessons too, but not
to the entire neglect of the soul, which here suffers
at the expense of the brain. Book-learning is
overdone here—that is my opinion. Everybody
wants to rise up and up so high through education
that finally manual labour becomes a disgrace;
too much importance is attached to knowledge and
culture.   Therefore it is not surprising if deference,
honesty, piety, and contentment yield to appalling ungodliness, scorn for everything sacred and
established, and the unscrupulous pursuit of
worldly advantages. With their outward education people's necessities increase, and their
demands upon life, hence the severity and the
bitterness of competition among them. Yes, the
mind is cultivated, to be sure, but the heart is left
untilled.   One should study the word of God and
His holy commandments first, speculating upon
"force and matter" last.

I was once dismayed to see by a statistical table of lunacy that the great majority of these unfortunates were recruited from former students at gymnasia and prominent institutions of learning. Undoubtedly, many had fallen into idiocy as victims of their ambitions striving after a fine education. I could not help thinking of my own country, where no lunatic asylums are wanted, and where I never heard of any maniacs but two, one a Negress and the other a woman from India.

European culture offends the Mahometan's religious views in countless ways. They often ridicule the Turkish half-education, yet the Turks have done more than is good for them to become civilised, if only superficially. The Turks have weakened themselves by those endeavours, in spite of which they have still remained uncivilised, because European civilisation contradicts and opposes all their fundamental axioms. You cannot produce civilisation by force, and you should allow other nations the right to follow their own ideas and traditions—which must have developed as the result of mature experience and practical wisdom—in seeking enlightenment after their own fashion. A pious Arab would feel deeply affronted were one to attempt beginning his illumination by inculcating science, without which there can be no question of higher culture in Europe. It would give him a terrible shock, it would convulse his mentality, if one spoke to him of "natural laws," to him who, in the whole life of the universe, down to the smallest details, through the eyes of his immutable faith sees only one thing—the all-guiding, all-governing hand of God!

CHAPTER VIII

Female Fashions

YEARLY DISTRIBUTION OF CLOTHING MATERIALS—
SIMPLE WANTS OF ARABIAN WOMEN—THE
SHALE—THE RAINY SEASON

HERE, and in Europe generally, the father of a family gives his wife and unmarried daughters an allowance of so much per month or quarter, and there his responsibilities end, so far as concerns their clothing. But a totally different state of affairs prevails in Zanzibar. We have no industries there, and consequently not a single factory. Wearing material and apparel are imported from abroad for the whole population.

My father maintained an elaborate system of barter, owing to this circumstance. Once a year a fleet of his sailing vessels laden with native products, especially cloves and spices, started for British, French, Persian, Indian, and Chinese ports, by means of our agents there employed exchanging the home commodities for foreign. The captains invariably took an enormously long list of articles required; most of which had something to do with clothes. The return of the ships, was of course awaited most eagerly and impatiently, since it meant not merely the annual division of spoils, but the opening, as it were, of a new season in fashions.

For us children those ships symbolised delightful mystery, as they brought us all our lovely toys from Europe. Upon the fleet's arrival a day would soon be fixed for the distribution of the goods among high and humble, old and young. Twenty or thirty boxes were full of playthings: horses, carts, dolls, whips, fishes and ducks that followed a magnet, musical boxes of all dimensions, concertinas, flutes, trumpets, mock guns, and what not. If we were displeased, woe to the delinquent captain; he was a plenipotentiary intrusted with full powers and no restrictions; he sailed under the one specific order to purchase the best regardless of expense.

When finally the division was enacted at Bet il Mtoni and Bet il Sahel, it took three or four days to get everything duly apportioned among several hundred persons. Eunuchs attended to the unpacking and sorting out, while a few of the Sultan's elder daughters performed the allotment proper. Jealousy, envy, and malice were unfortunately more conspicuous on this happy occasion than at any other time of the year. Materials for dress, whether simple or costly, were only distributed by the whole piece, and one was free to change what one did not want for a different article with somebody else. This trafficking might occupy

Photograph by A. C. Gomes & Co., Zanzibar

PICKING CLOVES FOR EXPORT

a fortnight. As we had no tables, we used to cut the pieces up sitting on the floor, and in eagerly plying the scissors a lady would now and then rip the clothes on her body.

Musk, amber, attar of roses, rose water, and other perfumes were presented to us, likewise saffron (which women mix with various ingredients to put in their hair), silks of all hues, gold and silver thread for embroidering, woven gilt buttons, in short, whatever belonged to an Arabian lady's toilette. And then, besides, each got a certain number of silver dollars, according to rank and age. But an extravagant individual would sometimes spend more, in the course of the twelvemonth, than she had received, when she would beg father or husband for an additional sum, although appeals of this kind had to be made under great secrecy, undue wastefulness being frowned upon, and moreover certain to bring down a lecture on the petitioner's head. As every household in the world, so ours included thrifty characters besides the prodigals, and they believed one should not keep slaves merely for luxury's sake, but should utilise them for one's substantial benefit. So they had their slaves trained to sundry handit crafts, such as carpentry or saddlery, the girls learning sewing, weaving, millinery. Of course, this proved a good method of economy, while those who neglected the practice paid out their money to strangers, and often failed to make both

ends meet. Slaves thus specially fitted for a trade
were thought more of than others, and if liberated
found less difficulty in sustaining life. In Oman,
where people keep few slaves, they are all taught
some regular profession, that they may profitably
serve both their masters and themselves. That
accounted for many slaves being sent from Zanzibar to Oman, to get training there, and Negroes
of this class went up considerably in price.

A visitor happening to be with us at the aforesaid period of distribution would receive such
share, cash included, as he or she might be entitled to by rank. Whatever was left from the
whole consignment the Sultan would despatch
to his kinsfolk in Oman.

Perpetual summer reigning at the equator,
and the four seasons existing in name only, this
decidedly simplified one's yearly outfit. To have
provided against autumn, winter, and spring into
the bargain would have entailed redoubtable com-
plications. The rainy season, which lasts six or
eight weeks, and during which the mercury sinks
to eighteen degrees Réaumur (about seventy-
two Fahrenheit), is all the winter that region ever
knows. Damp rather than cold, the weather
just now mentioned saw us in velvet and other
heavy stuffs, and instead of waiting for the nine
o'clock breakfast we then took tea with biscuits
an hour or two before.

All wearing apparel was made by hand; sewing

machines had not been heard of in my youth. The garments are cut quite plainly, the same way for either sex. Lacing, that injurious, abominable habit, is one to which the Oriental female has not yet succumbed. Styles never vary, but only materials, so that a European would complain of monotony; nevertheless, in Europe the continued changes of fashion cause family quarrels and ugly scenes owing to the great expense involved. Not that I would presume to reform this fashion craze, nor that I would wish to turn my enlightened European friends into Philistines; but I merely ask permission to observe that the Arabian women are far less extravagant. They use fewer things, and dispense with a winter coat or cloak, another for spring, a waterproof for summer, a host of dresses, a dozen or so of hats (for some ladies need one hat per costume), several sunshades matching hats and dresses, etc., etc.

Now, the gear of an Arab female, no matter what her station, is simplicity itself. She wears a shirt reaching to the ankles, a pair of long, wide trousers gathered above the foot—not short knickerbockers—and a kerchief for the head. The materials vary. Rich women prefer gold brocades in many devices, velvet or silk richly trimmed, but in very hot weather plain, light calico or muslin is worn. Shirt and trousers never conform as to pattern. Neither may the shirt be too long, for it must not conceal the embroidery on the trousers or the golden anklets, from one of which are suspended numerous little bell-shaped pieces of gold producing an agreeable tinkle at every step. From the headband, which is wound about the forehead, two long ribbons with large fringes hang together over the back or one down each side. The silk headkerchief proper reaches as far as the ankles.

When an Arabian lady goes out she dons her *shale*, representing comforter, jacket, ulster, waterproof, and dustcoat all in one. It is a large wrap made of black silk, worked round the edges with gold or silver designs according to the owner's prosperity and taste; but neither a rich woman nor a poor has more than one *shale*, and its style never alters. My humble opinion is that an Oriental, with all her leisure, and her inactivity enforced through the heat, has a better excuse to devote much interest to her clothes than the bright, busy European, and I must say it baffles me how such clever people, with such high mental development, can absorb themselves so completely in trivialities of that kind.

During the rainy season the well-to-do put on a *djocha*, a sort of long cape coming down to the feet, and richly embroidered in gilt. This is worn, indoors, over everything else; open from top to bottom, the *djocha* is held together at the chest by means of metal clasps. Elderly ladies prefer a thick Persian shawl.

However, we were prepared for all contingencies in the possession of a very convenient heating apparatus. A brass tripod standing a few inches above the floor was filled with glowing charcoal, and placed in the middle of the room, diffusing an agreeable warmth. This, too, was the season of the maize harvest. The cobs are peeled, and put on the tripod to roast, so that they become eatable in about five minutes. Meanwhile the grains would continually be going "pop!"—a fine diversion for us children. Despite the miniature stove, doors and windows were as a rule left open.

CHAPTER IX

The Sultan's Voyage to Oman

PERSIAN HOSTILITY IN ASIA—PROVISIONING THE
SHIPS—RELATIVES IN OMAN—DIFFICULTIES OF
CORRESPONDING WITH THEM—THE DEPARTURE
—KHALED REPRESENTS SEYYID SAID—CHOLE
AS LADY SUPERINTENDENT—THE SULTAN'S
STRANGELY PROLONGED ABSENCE — RESORT
TO PROFESSIONAL SEERS—SOOTHSAYING BY
VENTRILOQUISM

WHEN I was about nine years old, the Sultan
took a journey to Oman, as he was in the habit
of doing at intervals of three of four years, to
regulate the government of his Asiatic realm.
My modest brother Tueni had been representing him
at Muscat, both as ruler and as head of the family.
On the present occasion my father's reasons for
visiting Oman included one that was particularly
urgent. The Persians had several times invaded
the region of Bender Abbas, without very serious
results, it is true, but yet not without the possibility of generating a war. Originally Persian,
this small territory of ours, important enough
through its commanding position at the entrance
to the gulf, never brought my father any real
advantage, but on the contrary, rich harvests of

MUSCAT IN THE MIDDLE OF THE 17TH CENTURY

As sketched by the Dutch traveller, Jan Struys

trouble and expense. So that its eventual recapture proved no misfortune; while the tract was in our possession the Persians left us not a moment free from anxiety, for which, after all, they could scarcely be blamed.

Having no steamers, but only sailing vessels to dispose of, we depended altogether on the caprices of the wind, and voyages from Zanzibar therefore frequently suffered postponement. The preparations consumed at least eight or ten weeks, since food had to be provided to meet the needs of a thousand people for a similar period. It took an immense time to bake the durable pastry that was required. Pickled meats were foreign to us, and preserves, even had we had any, would have been forbidden as unclean by our religion; hence a stupendous number of live cattle were taken on board, among them perhaps a dozen milch cows. The quantities of fruit enshipped defies my calculation, but I know that all our forty-five plantations kept sending fruit for days. Small wonder if dysentery broke out on these voyages.

Any of the sons might go, but only a few of the daughters, because of the inconvenience, for which reason no more than a couple of the secondary wives could embark. Not many of us, in fact, cared to visit Oman, whose conceited women liked to treat natives of Zanzibar as inferiors. Members of our family born in Oman would exhibit this attitude toward their Zanzibar re-

lations, assuming that we must resemble Negroes
from having been brought up among them. Our
most obvious patent of degradation was our
speaking another language besides Arabic.

As I mentioned before, we had needy connections
living in Oman, to whom a visit by the Sultan
meant the arrival of gifts, and this expectation
caused a further increase of the luggage. His
journey would also revive our slim, infrequent
correspondence with Asia. Ignorance of writing,
however proved a serious difficulty in many cases.
Your letters had to be written for you by someone
else, and then strangers would read them to their
recipients. My brothers and the male servants
who had acquired penmanship were besieged, and
if they refused you had no choice but to ask somebody outside the house. The following is an
example of the sort of thing that might happen:

A lady summons her confidential slave, and
says to him: "Now, Feruz, go to such and such
a *cadi;* tell him to write a fine letter to my friend in
Oman, and pay him anything he asks." Feruz is
then given copious details, all of these to be em-
bodied in the letter. Unfortunately the cadi is
pressed and importuned by a dozen other would-be
correspondents at the same time, so that he mixes
up his commissions. Feruz returns triumphantly
to his mistress with the cadi's effort, but the lady
is cautious enough to make an expert read it out
to her. Surprise is the first emotion that seizes

her, and dismay follows quickly. The epistle is conceived wrong in every respect; where the lady intended condolence the cadi has expressed congratulation and so on. Thus a letter must be written several times over by sundry individuals before it can be sent.

At last all was ready for departure. One vessel was reserved for my father and members of his family; the retinue and luggage were to go in two or three other ships. The number of travellers was considerable in proportion to the ships; still, the Oriental does not take up much room: he demands no separate cabin, but when night falls he selects a place on deck, where he spreads out his mat. The Sultan's suite and the servants embarked first; early in the morning came the women's turn; about the middle of the day followed Seyyid Saïd and his male relations. My brothers Khaled and Majid, I recollect, went down to the shore with some of their younger brothers to see the Sultan off, a salute of twenty-one guns celebrating the start.

A hush seemed to fall on the house, which now felt solitary—though densely populated—without its head. Khaled, as the Sultan's eldest son in Zanzibar, was to represent him during his absence. He came to our house several times a week to enquire about us, and went to Bet il Mtoni as often to see the inmates, and to consult our high and mighty stepmother, Azze bint Sef.

Khaled was a strict master; we had frequent cause to resent his severity.

One day a fire broke out at Bet il Sahel, which was fortunately extinguished without delay. But when it began, and we all ran panic-stricken to the doors, we found them locked and guarded by soldiers. They had been ordered there by Khaled, who wished to prevent us from exposing ourselves to the popular gaze in broad daylight. Another time he turned a distant but influential connection out of a mosque for having dared to propose for the hand of one of his sisters. The unhappy suitor ventured neither into Khaled's presence again, nor into the mosque where he prayed. Fate ordained, however, that after Khaled's and Seyyid Saïd's deaths the rejected one was to marry another sister.

For the period of his absence my father had nominated Chole as lady superintendent—if I may use such a term—over the two houses Bet il Sahel and Bet il Tani. The appointment of this bright star of our family aroused great disapproval, due to envy, of course. Her kindness of heart notwithstanding, she was unable to please everybody, since she was only mortal like the rest of us. The impossible was expected of her, the limits of her delegated power being ignored; it was clearly not her fault if she was favoured by the Sultan, but envy blinded intelligence.

Meanwhile our three-masters sailed to and fro

WATER-FRONT OF MAJID'S CAPITAL

between Oman and Zanzibar, so that we often received news and gifts from the Sultan. The arrival of a ship naturally occasioned great joy; the excitement, the tumult, and the wild gesticulating were of a kind to be seen nowhere but in the South. Sad to relate, Khaled was soon taken away by the Lord. The regency was transferred to Majid, who was entitled to it, as the Sultan's next son, and whose amiable disposition had won all hearts.

Finally a ship came in from Oman with the glad tidings that the Sultan was coming back. The news spread quickly, and the whole island was overjoyed; his absence having lasted over two years, my father had been greatly missed. Whoever did not feel genuine devotion toward him at least anticipated his return with pleasure on account of the presents he would be sure to bring old and young in Zanzibar. Yet after the lapse of a period sufficient to allow for the voyagers' arrival, not a single ship had heaved in sight. People grew alarmed both in town and country. Now, the Arab is addicted to questioning so-called "seers" about the hidden future, and in Zanzibar as well as among the Suahilis this abuse runs riot. Gipsies might learn a lot from their Suahili brethren; they practise an appalling amount of deception which, on the other hand, is met with astonishing credulity. Any means of gaining an explanation as to the Sultan's protracted journey were considered legitimate, and thus the talented individuals I have mentioned came down upon us by the score. They were fetched from all parts of the island, even the remotest; if they happened to be very old, they were brought in on donkeys.

Of the most remarkable of these prophetesses it was said that she, or rather her yet unborn child, could forecast future events, and this unparalleled monstrosity was accordingly sent for. I remember the day she appeared quite distinctly. Her stoutness was abnormal. The child that she professed to have been carrying about in her womb for years was a wonder of omniscience: nothing that occurred on the heights of the mountains or in the depths of the seas was concealed from it. Some asked it how the Sultan was faring, and why his voyage was taking so long. The reply came in a small, piping voice, plainly. Several three-masters, the creature proclaimed, were on the ocean, steering for Zanzibar. It would light upon the Sultan's ship, it said, to ascertain what was doing there. And in a little while it gave a detailed account of everyone's particular activity at that moment. Then it commanded a liberal sacrifice to propitiate the spirits of the water, that they might watch over the travellers and keep them from harm.

Of course the prodigy was obeyed to the letter; for several days professional beggars—our beautiful island harbours legions of them—revelled in the meat, poultry, and rice dealt out to them, to say nothing of clothes and money. We eventually discovered, to our intense disgust, that we had been victimised by a ventriloquist. We had all believed in the marvellous child, with its capacity to disclose the unseen, to reveal secrets hidden from the human eye. But at the time none of us suspected ventriloquism, because we had up till then never heard of such a thing. The occult and the mysterious attract the natives of Zanzibar irresistibly; the less comprehensible a circumstance, the more probable its reality. Everybody believes in invisible spirits, good and evil. The room in which a person has died is thoroughly fumigated with incense for days, and since the soul of the departed is supposed to be fond of visiting the erstwhile sick-chamber, that place is studiously avoided, especially at night, when no one could be induced to go there at any price.

Superstition reigns supreme. Illness, betrothal, pregnancy, and all sorts of reasons are given for summoning seers. They are asked if a disease be curable, and how long it is likely to last; whether a betrothal will be smiled upon by fortune; whether a boy or a girl may be expected—and so forth. In the event of her prediction turning out wrong, which happens quite frequently, the prophetess always musters a plausible excuse.

The day was an unlucky one for her, she alleges, and no doubt she will do better next time.   Which goes down beautifully! The trade is so profitable that whoever engages in it may soon hope to become a made man—or rather, a made woman.

CHAPTER X

Death of Seyyid Saïd

PREPARATIONS FOR THE SULTAN'S RETURN—MAJID
SETS OUT TO MEET HIM—THE PALACE SUR-
ROUNDED BY ORDER OF BARGASH—WHO WANTS
TO USURP THE THRONE—ARRIVAL OF THE
SULTAN'S DEAD BODY—MAJID'S RETURN—
COURT MOURNING—MAJID'S IRREGULAR SUC-
CESSION—SEVERANCE OF ZANZIBAR FROM OMAN
—DIVISION OF SEYYID SAÏD'S PROPERTY

DAYS and weeks went by, and the Sultan did
not arrive. One afternoon, at length, while some
were still at prayer, the good news was reported
that a fisherman had descried several ships flying
our national flag, although owing to the rough
weather he had not ventured out very far. Of
course this must be the Sultan returning! So all
threw themseves into their best finery, long held
in readiness for the joyous event.

While we made the fisherman repeat his state-
ments over and again, and swear as many times
to their veracity, a mounted messenger was
despatched to our stepmother at Bet il Mtoni.
In the courtyard commenced butchering and
boiling and baking, the apartments were sprinkled
with perfumes, and everything was arranged to

look perfect. According to the fisherman's version, the vessels were due in a couple of hours. Majid hastened, with an escort, to meet his father. They went in two cutters, fighting the storm which threatened their destruction, and expecting to be in our midst again that evening accompanied by Seyyid Saïd.

Night fell, and not a ship was seen. The town, and especially our house, began to show disquietude, then loud alarm. It was supposed that Majid and his escort had perished in the tempest, but this apprehension grew into a fear that the whole fleet had sunk to the bottom. Presentiments were exchanged against surmises, and vice versa, while nobody, down to the infants, would go to bed without learning of the travellers' safe landing.

Suddenly a rumour sprung up which at first obtained no credence, to the effect that the palace was surrounded and guarded by soldiers. We all rushed to the windows to ascertain the truth. The night was dark as pitch, but you could occasionally see the barrel of a gun glisten, which sight was not exactly soothing in its effect upon a lot of nervous women and frightened children. Besides, we were given to understand that the soldiers had established a blockade of the house allowing neither entrance not departure. What had happened, and why we had been shut up, everybody was clamouring to know, but uppermost was the question as to who had originated these proceedings. Majid, so far as we knew, was not back; moreover, people were hastening to and fro uneasily in his house, which was guarded like ours.

As the eunuchs and all male slaves slept outside our residence, the women and children were the more terrified. A few of the bravest women betook themselves to the hall on the ground floor, where they could speak to the soldiers through the windows. The troops however proved obdurate, abiding by their instructions to give no information; in fact they went so far as to threaten to shoot the noisiest servants. Weeping lamentations accused an evil demon; children screamed, and could not be quieted; pious souls prayed to the Almighty. In short, the scene was indescribable, and one suddenly transplanted amid the horrible confusion of that dreadful night must have thought himself in a lunatic asylum.

Morning dawned, and still we were left in ignorance as to why we had been imprisoned; nor did we hear anything of Majid. But as we were dispersing, at the regular hour for prayer, someone exclaimed that the fleet lay anchored in the harbour with mourning flags displayed. Then our brothers came—without the Sultan. And then we understood what the mourning on the ships signified, and what an irreparable loss the nation had sustained; for during the voyage from Oman to Zanzibar that faithful servant of

the Lord had been called to the eternal rest. The
bullet wound in his leg, that had tormented him
so long, had done its fatal work. Not only was
the deceased the devoted father of his family
and people, but the most conscientious of rulers,
How generally he was loved was shown at his
death, when every house, down to the humblest
cottage, exhibited a black flag.

Bargash, who had travelled in our father's
vessel, and had witnessed his death, gave us the
sad particulars. We owed thanks to Bargash
for saving the precious corpse from burial in the
ocean, which would have conformed with the
Mahometan religion; he had insisted upon bringing the body back to Zanzibar, in fact, ordering
a sort of coffin to be made on board for its preservation. Though actuated by profound sentiments
toward his father, he here commited a grave
offence against our religious doctrines and customs. We do not acknowledge the use of coffins,
we believe that everybody, prince and pauper
alike, ought to go back in a natural state to the
earth whence he came.

Now we discovered, too, why we had been so
carefully guarded the night before. Majid, in
his frail little craft, had been driven hither and
thither by the storm, and had so missed Bargash,
who—in command of the fleet as the Sultan's
senior survivor at sea—had landed the corpse
unobserved in order to bury it secretly in our

Copyright by Maull & Fox, London

SEYYID BARGASH
Ruled from 1870 to 1888

cemetery. Tradition orders that in case of a dispute about the succession, the matter shall be settled publicly in the presence of the deceased. Bargash, however, desired to seize the reins of power himself; he knew that if the prescribed ceremonial debate took place, his elder brother Majid would prove a universal favourite, and therefore concluded to forestall any such result. So, directly after landing he had caused the two houses to be surrounded. His scheme failed because he did not catch Majid, who had not yet returned. Bargash subsequently tried to justify his proceedings on the ground that he wanted to avert the possibility of a revolution.

Majid thus became ruler of Zanzibar, proclaiming himself Sultan that very day. The rest of us felt uneasy doubts as to how long Majid would keep the sovereignty; for our eldest brother, Tueni, who had remained in Oman, and was entitled to the throne, might come to take it away from Majid by force.

On going into mourning for Seyyid Saïd we all had to discard our fine clothes, and put on coarse black woollen garments; the handsomely embroidered veils gave way to veils of a plain black material. Anointing and scenting of the person was stopped; whoever sprinkled a little rosewater on her apparel, to counteract the disagreeable smell of the indigo dye, was denounced as heartless or coquettish. The first few days the grown-up people slept on the floor, and not in bed, in order to show their regard for the deceased, who lay on the hard ground, A full fortnight did our house resemble a huge hotel, while anybody, beggar or prince, was at liberty to come and eat "ad libitum." In obedience to an old tradition, the Sultan's favourite dish especially was cooked in large quantities, and put before the poor.

The wives of a dead Sultan, principal as well as secondary, are without exception obliged to submit to a period of religious mourning, which lasts four months. These unfortunates must spend the whole time in a dark room; they must never purposely expose themselves to the light of day, let alone the sunshine. If a widow is for some reason compelled to leave her artificially darkened room, she throws a heavy black cloth over her veil, so that she can just manage to grope her way. The eyes become affected by this confinement, and some caution must afterward be used in accustoming them to the light. At the beginning, the women are reminded by the cadi, that is to say the judge, or magistrate, before whom they of course appear densely muffled, of their widowhood in certain set phrases. When the four months are over the same official ends their rigid seclusion by other verbal formalities.

At this date, too, my father's widows had simultaneously to undergo a complete washing, from head to foot. Throughout its duration a servant stood behind each, beating a pair of sword-blades together above her mistress's head. (In the case of a poor man's widow a pair of nails, or anything of iron, was permissible.)   Owing to the large number of wives left by my father, this ceremony could not be accomplished at the baths, extensive though they were, but had to be performed on the shore, which afforded a strange and animated spectacle. The widows were now allowed to change their costume, and to consider themselves eligible for remarriage.   Ordinarily the Sultan's wives were visible at home to all their male relations and their own male servants, but during the four months no men except their brothers and step-brothers might see them.

The first year following his death, some of us would repair to Seyyid Saïd's grave each Thursday, the eve of the Mahometan Sunday.   His tomb was a rectangular structure covered with a large cupola, where several of my brothers and sisters reposed.   After reciting the first *sura* of the Koran, and then other prayers, beseeching the Almighty to forgive the departed their sins, we poured attar of roses and rosewater upon their resting places, which we also scented with amber and musk, all the while giving vent to loud lamentations over our loss.   Mahometans believe firmly in the immortality of the soul; they likewise believe that the spirits of the dead occasionally visit (unseen) their living friends, who acknowledge this interest by devotions at the graves. Briefly, the dead are profoundly revered; when a Mahometan of good reputation swears by the head or the name of one departed, you know that he would sooner perish than break his oath.

A ship having been despatched to Oman for the purpose of announcing the sorrowful calamity that had befallen us, my brother Muhammad, representing all my brothers and sisters in Oman, arrived at Zanzibar to supervise the apportionment of the heritage. Hardly was his task done, when he sped back to Muscat without delay. Muhammad was accounted the most pious member of our whole family; from his youth up he had sought to eschew the world and its affairs. Hostile to riches and outward show, he never enjoyed his position as prince. The more displeasing did he find the luxury of the court at Zanzibar, particularly as Oman knew no such splendours. He felt positively unhappy surrounded by all the magnificence, whence his haste to resume his wonted simpler life.

The question of succession was not properly settled. Majid, who reigned in our island, cared not at all whether Tueni, who assumed rulership over Oman, acknowledged him as Sultan of Zanzibar, which in fact Tueni never did. Eventually a sort of compromise was patched up through British influence, Majid binding himself to pay

his elder brother a yearly sum; however Majid
only kept to the agreement for a short time,
ceasing the payment because it might appear as
tribute from a vassal. Tueni was helpless; he
had enough to contend with at home, and was far
too poor to assert his rights against the prosperous
lord of Zanzibar by means of an armed expedition.
Sans pact, *sans* treaty, Zanzibar and Oman parted
company, either existing thenceforth as an independent state. On the other hand, Muhammad contrived a satisfactory division of my
father's private fortune in Zanzibar. The "State,"
as it is understood by Europeans, means nothing
in Zanzibar. National income and national revenue being unknown there, everything levied by
way of imposts was my father's own personal
property. Out of this and the income derived
from his forty-five plantations—he was the principal landlord of the island—he fed his treasury
and met expenses. In my day, at least, there
was neither an income tax, nor a ground tax, nor
any industrial tax of the kind familiar here.

My father's whole private property, then, was
divided up, even the warships going to Tueni and
Majid between them. The Mahometan law favours
the sons above the daughters in cases of legacies,
for the reason that a man must support a family,
which a woman is not obliged to do. Each of my
sisters therefore got only half as much as each
brother. My brother Ralub, once my playmate

at Bet il Mtoni, and I were declared of age, although neither was more than twelve. This contradicted the usual practice, but the occasion brought peculiar changes. Both of us received our part in the inheritance, and so became emancipated citizens of twelve. Our younger brothers and sisters and their share remained under Majid's keeping and control.

My father's will ordered his childless wives to be provided for until they died, the mothers of his children getting but relatively small lump sums. He must have presumed that we would take care of our mothers, since we inherited vastly more than they did. Nor did he judge us wrongly, for I can answer, to the credit and honour of all my brothers and sisters—thirty-six survived my father—that not one abused his tacit confidence. A mother is a mother, whether born princess or purchased slave, and without regard to money or station she has every claim to filial attachment.

Soon after the legacy was disposed of our once overpopulated establishment grew lonely and deserted, at any rate in comparison to former days. Many of my brothers and sisters left Bet il Sahel with their mothers and slaves of both sexes to found homes of their own. Chole, Assha, and Shewane not following suit, my mother and I stayed on with them at Bet il Tani. At Bet il Mtoni things altered too in a similar manner. It

ALI BIN HAMUD
Present Sultan of Zanzibar. Acceded in 1902

was indeed right that some of us who now had resources, and were free to choose our own mode of life, should relieve the pressure of space by surrendering the large houses to our younger brothers and sisters.   Of the junior children, their mothers, and their servants, Majid took charge, of course defraying all expenditure from their incomes.

CHAPTER XI

THE POSITION OF WOMAN IN THE EAST

UNHAPPY WESTERN MATCHES—SECLUSION FROM
THE MALE SEX—POLYGAMY AND MONOGAMY—
CONSIDERATION TOWARD WIVES—REDRESS
AGAINST HUSBANDS—DOMESTIC PREROGATIVES
OF THE WOMEN—THEIR CHEERFULNESS—IM-
PENETRABILITY OF THE HAREM—DIVORCE EASY
—EXAMPLES DISPROVING THE "INFERIORITY"
OF ORIENTAL WOMEN.

I PASS on to write about the position of woman
in the East. As I was born and bred there, I
shall be considered a partisan and shall probably
not succeed in demolishing the erroneous views
prevailing throughout Europe, and especially
among Germans, as to the relations between an
Arabian wife and her husband.

When first I came to Europe I too made the
mistake of judging by outward appearances.
The smiling faces I saw each time I went out into
company persuaded me that the domestic situation in Europe was more conducive to happiness
than in my home. But later on, as my children
grew up, and needed less of my care and attention
I came into fuller contact with the world; then I
recognised that I had been mistaken, that people

and things were other than they seemed. I observed many unions, which going by the name of wedlock, had the apparent purpose of subjecting the fettered couples to infernal torture here on earth. And I have seen enough wretched marriages to prevent my believing that the Christian institution stands much higher than the Mahometan, or insures much greater felicity. Neither a religion, nor the acceptance of traditional views can guarantee wedded bliss; everything depends on how well husband and wife understand one another. This alone can bring the peace and harmony which render marriage really delightful. I am minutely familiar only with conditions in Zanzibar, though almost equally so with those of Oman. Yet precisely in Arabia and among the Arabs has Mahometanism been maintained in its purest form, and I may therefore claim to speak for the Mahometan Orient generally—leaving aside those parts of it tainted by excrescences arising from close intercourse with the Christian Occident.

To commence with: it is wrong to suppose that the Eastern woman enjoys less social respect than her husband. A man's principal wife—the bought secondary wives are of course not under discussion —is the husband's equal in every way, keeping her rank and its attendant rights and privileges. What makes the Arabian woman appear helpless and to some extent restricted in her freedom is the circumstance of her leading a retired life. This she does in all Mahometan countries of the East, and in some that are not Mahometan, and the loftier her station the stricter the rule. Her face may be seen by no men excepting father, husband, sons, uncles, nephews, and her own slaves; if she is to go into the presence of a strange man, or to speak with one, the faith ordains that she be veiled and covered up. Part of the visage, chin, neck, and ankles must be concealed. Obedient to this law, she may move about as she pleases, and frequent the streets. Females of small means, who have few servants or none, are obliged to go out frequently, and they thus have more liberty. If you ask such a woman her opinion she says those laws were not made for poor people. And I must avow that ladies of position are known to envy poorer women this advantage, which accrues to those of Oman because they cannot keep many servants in their unprosperous country.

However, the rich woman may go out in the daytime. Should a relative fall ill or die she may go to the house, or she may appear before a judge to represent her own interests, as there are no attorneys. But tradition ordains that she make no use of this privilege except under urgent necessity; inclination seconds tradition, for vanity causes the women to dislike covering themselves up and resembling walking dummies. Although I admit that the Oriental view is extravagant, I find European notions of dress no improvement; the costume worn here by ladies at balls seems to indicate still worse exaggeration in the opposite direction.

A woman without male connections is indeed to be pitied. Shut off entirely from the stronger sex by religion and custom, and therefore lacking advice and protection, she may get into sore straits; she is apt to be fleeced by her steward, and otherwise cheated. Indeed, several of my acquaintances married to escape from being constantly tricked. So that the enforced seclusion of women may go far enough to become extremely onerous. Nevertheless, the Eastern woman stands in no need of all the sympathy showered upon her in Europe; she does not feel the restriction much, for habit makes any life tolerable.

She is yet more commiserated because of polygamy, because she is forced to share her husband's love with another or others. The Moslem is allowed four wives by law, and if one dies or obtains a divorce he can take a fifth; secondary wives he may buy as many as he cares to. But I never saw a man who had four regular wives at once; a poor man can afford only one, and a rich man does not go beyond two, who live apart, each having her own establishment. Some women maintain their independence, demanding of a suitor that he sign a contract binding himself neither to marry nor buy anyone else.

In practice, then, monogamy is predominant.
But if a man avails himself of his legal rights to
the full, a painful state of affairs is apt to result.
Naturally enough hatred and malice step in, and
the hot Southern blood boils up in furious jealousy
—whose frequent manifestation should tend to
prove how much more ardently the Oriental loves
than her calmer Northern sister. Through the
passion of jealousy polygamous life often renders
itself unendurable, and that is well. Many an
affluent man balks at the daily scenes and quarrels, preferring the one-wife system to such a
contingency. That polygamy admits of neither
defence nor excuse every person able to think
intelligently, and especially every woman, must
plainly see.

But what about marriage among Christians,
among civilised Europeans? I pass over the
polygamy, existing under the name of Mormonism
with a Christian sect in a Christian land. Coming
to respectable society in Europe, is wedlock really
such a sacred institution? Is it not often absurd
to speak of "one" wife? True, the Christian
dispensation permits but a single mate, and that
is a great blessing. Christianity commands the
good and the right, Mahometanism allowing
evil. Yet the prevailing customs and actualities
of Oriental life mitigate the bad consequences of
the law to an appreciable degree, while here sin
very frequently takes the upper hand in spite of

the law. Almost the sole difference between an Oriental woman's situation and a Western woman's seems to be that the first knows the number and perhaps the disposition and character of her rivals, whereas the other is kept in charming ignorance.

Of course none but wealthy men can afford to purchase secondary wives. Slaves at the beginning, motherhood insures them emancipation. In rare cases cruel masters will sell them after the child's death, from satiety or for the money's sake. Upon a man's decease all his secondary wives become free. If one of them then makes a match with a brother or other relation of her former master, she does so as a regular, that is, a principal wife.

That the Arab treats nis partner contemptuously is a myth. Our creed alone would prevent this, and if by its terms woman is in some respects rated man's inferior, she is at the same time recommended to his protection because of her weakness. A devout, God-fearing Moslem displays just as much kindness as a well-bred, cultivated European, perhaps even governs himself with more rigour, since he never forgets the omnipresence of the Lord, nor till his last breath relinquishes his firm belief in Divine retribution. Of course, you find wretches everywhere who deny their wives the proper amiability and consideration, but I can conscientiously affirm that here I have heard more of tender husbands who beat their wives than at home; a good Arab would think he was dishonouring himself did he thus transgress. With the Negroes the matter stands differently on the plantations. I have often interfered and made peace between a pair lustily belabouring each other.

Nor is a woman subject to all her consort's whims. If one of them offends her she may seek support with her relatives, or she is entitled, if alone in the world, to apply for justice to the cadi. Sometimes she fights her own battle. An intimate friend of mine at sixteen accepted the hand of a much older cousin, who was quite unworthy of her. Thoroughly devil-may-care, he imagined his wife would endure anything; consequently his surprise was great, upon returning home one night, to find her absent and a message couched in strong language awaiting him instead. I had been in the habit of visiting my friend on her estate without giving notice, for I knew her delightful spouse preferred the pleasures of the town. But one day she came to tell me I must visit her no more without previous announcement, as her husband was now always at home, He had gone after her repentantly, and implored her pardon; having once discovered how resolute she was, he took good care not to affront her again. I might quote other examples of female independence.

When a married couple meet they kiss one

another's hands. Their meals they eat together
with the children. A woman does sundry little
works of love for her husband; when he goes out
she hands him his weapons, relieves him of them
upon his return, proffers him drinking water, and
so forth, performs, in short, those trifling attentions which render common existence pleasant
and happy—and does so without an atom of
compulsion. In domestic management she reigns
supreme. A special allowance for housekeeping
is not in vogue, man and wife drawing upon the
same purse, though if a man has two principal
wives with separate establishments he divides his
income. To what extent a woman will assert
her domestic prerogatives varies according to her
disposition and her husband's. Once, when I
was giving a large party on a plantation of mine,
and a number of refusals seemed imminent because
of the difficulty of procuring mounts in time, a
lady offered to lend me all the donkeys and drivers
I might want. Upon my suggestion that she
obtain her husband's consent to this generous
proposal, she replied rather curtly that she was
not accustomed to asking his sanction in such
unimportant matters. Another of my Zanzibar
acquaintances had yet wider control over domestic
and economic affairs, managing his country estates
and his town houses. He did not even know the
amount of his revenues, neither did he object
to receiving from her hand whatever money he

needed, and owing to her cleverness and far-sightedness he came off very well.

The bringing up of children lies entirely in the mother's hands, be she a regular wife or an acquired slave, and therein she is most fortunate. While a fashionable Englishwoman is expected to look into the nursery once every twenty-four hours, and a Frenchwoman sends her offspring to the country, where they are taken charge of by strangers, the Arabian tends hers with minute care and circumstance, scarcely letting them out of her sight so long as they require motherly tutelage. Intense love, deep respect, are her reward; her relations with her little ones compensate her for the detriments of polygamy. making her family life happy and enjoyable. One who has witnessed the lightheartedness and mirthfulness of Eastern women must known how little truth resides in all the stories of their oppression and degradation, and of their listless, futile dreaming.

But a profound insight of the real conditions is not to be gained through a visit counting minutes. All his courtesy notwithstanding, the Arab does not like outsiders—particularly if they belong to a foreign nation or creed—spying into his private concerns. When a European arrived to see us we would begin by staring at her tremendous circumference, as in that day crinolines were worn which filled the width of a staircase.

The conversation was scant, and usually confined to the mysteries of dress. After the lady had been shown the customary hospitalities, scented with rosewater by a eunuch, and presented with farewell gifts, she would depart no wiser than when she came. She had been in the harem, seen the "unfortunate" inmates (veiled), wondered at our costume, our jewellery, our agility in sitting down on the floor—and that was all. Never could she boast of finding out anything beyond other Europeans who had visited us. She would be attended from and to the door by eunuchs; she would not be unwatched for an instant. A Westerner is rarely shown any apartment but that she is received in; she sometimes fails to make out the veiled lady entertaining her. Briefly, she gets no opportunity to investigate Oriental family life and the standing of our women.

Another point regarding matrimony: a girl's entering the wedded estate does not alter her rank or name. A prince's wife sprung from simple folk would never think of claiming titular equality with him; despite the union she remains "daughter of So-and-So," and is thus addressed. Contrariwise, an Arab prince or chieftain often allows a daughter or sister to marry his own slave; he says to himself; my servant is her servant, and therefore she stays his mistress as before. However, at such a marriage he ceases from being a slave in the proper sense, though he speaks to his wife as "highness" or "mistress" as a matter of course. A man alluding to his wife in conversation—which he preferably avoids—never refers to her as "my wife," but designates her as "daughter of So-and-So"; or he may say "mother of my family," whether she has children or not.

A couple unacquainted before marriage sometimes find agreement difficult or impossible, and the Mahometan rule of easy divorce hence proves undoubtedly beneficial. Surely it is better that a pair radically differing in opinions and character should separate peacefully than be chained together for their whole lives, to their mutual torment, perhaps culminating in an outburst of violence or crime. A woman then gets her property back, over which she has had unrestricted control all along. If the husband applies for divorce she retains his wedding gift, but surrenders it if divorce takes place at her instigation.

From all I have written above it must clearly appear that the Oriental woman is no such wronged and oppressed creature, no such zero, as she is reported to be. My stepmother Azze bint Sef's example is significant. She held complete sway over Seyyid Saïd, with court and state direction bent to her caprices. Did one of us wish to obtain anything from the Sultan the request had to be approved by her, and she preserved her power until his death.

Another case I remember is that of the daughter

of a military officer belonging to Oman. She came with her husband to live in Zanzibar; she was sharp and witty; yet hideously plain. Nevertheless he adored her, meeting her fads and fancies with angelic patience. Willy-nilly, he was obliged to escort her wheresoever she went, and not a moment of his time could he safely count upon as his own. He was simply her slave.

I have still another personage to mention in disproof of the fiction as the Eastern woman's "inferiority." To this day my great aunt—sister to my grandfather—is thought of as a model of shrewdness, courage, and efficiency.

Upon the death of my grandfather, the ruler of Oman, known as Imam of Muscat, three children survived, my father Saïd, my uncle Selim, and my aunt Assha. My father being nine years old, a regency had to be established, when my great aunt, contrary to all precedent, declared she would herself govern until her nephew reached his majority, and overruled the objectors. The ministers, who had been anticipating the pleasure of governing the country to suit their own plans, were greatly disappointed, but had to obey. Every day they were obliged to appear before the regent, to make their reports and receive orders. She kept an eye on everybody, and seemed to know about everything, to the chagrin of the idle and the negligent. The bonds of etiquette

she cast off arbitrarily. When she consulted with
her ministers she wore her *shale*, as if she had been
going out, quite indifferent to the world's critic-
isms, and intent upon accomplishing her task
with prudence and energy.

She had not been reigning long when war broke
out, a lamentably frequent occurrence in Oman.
A clan related to ours wanted to upset the government, and seize upon it for themselves—an
easy matter, they thought, in view of the petticoat
rulership. So, devastating the country with fire
and sword, they marched as far as Muscat, and
laid siege to it, having driven into that town a
lot of peasants fleeing before them, and seeking
shelter and succour. Muscat is strongly fortified,
but what avail the thickest walls if food and
ammunition run short?

It was now that my aunt showed the stuff she
was made of, gaining even the admiration of the
enemy. At night she would ride forth in men's
clothes to inspect the outposts, and sometimes
escaped capture only through the swiftness of her
horse. One evening she rode out in very low
spirits, for she had learned that the enemy intended to try bribery with the purpose of breaking
into the fortress, and slaying the whole garrison.
Determining to put the fidelity of her troops to
the test, she approached a sentinel, asked for his
superior, and offered a tempting inducement in
the name of the opposite side. The wrath of this

gallant soldier reassured her, though she was nearly killed for a spy by her own adherents.

Muscat's plight went from bad to worse. Famine started, and general gloom set in. No assistance being expected from without, it was decided at least to die honourably, and to make a final, desperate sortie. There was just enough powder left for one battle; on the other hand, there was no more lead. Then the Regent commanded that all nails be gathered, and even pebbles of the right size, to make ammunition for the muskets; all other objects of iron or brass were broken up, and cast into cannon ball; yes, even the silver dollars in the treasury were sacrificed—they were melted into bullets. And these extreme measures resulted in success. Taken by surprise, the hostile force scattered to the four points of the compass, leaving half their number behind as dead or wounded. Muscat was saved.

My great aunt continued to govern unmolested after that, and the realm was in such perfect order when she handed it over to my father, that he was able to cast his eyes abroad in search of new conquerable territory—Zanzibar. That we ever acquired this second domain was therefore largely due to her.

And she was an Oriental woman!

CHAPTER XII

Arabian Suitorship and Marriage

FIRST ACQUAINTANCE—GENERALLY BY HEARSAY
—GIRLS FREE TO REJECT SUITORS—FOR-
MALITIES TO BE OBSERVED BY THE
BRIDE—WEDDING RITES

AMONG the Arabs a matrimonial union is
generally arranged by the father or the head of
the family. Nor is there anything peculiar about
this; it frequently happens in Europe, where
extreme liberty of intercourse exists between the
sexes. How often do we not hear of a reckless
spendthrift, so deeply in debt that the only way
out is to sacrifice a beautiful or charming daughter
to his creditor; or of a frivolous, worldly woman
positively driving her child into an unhappy
marriage simply to get rid of her at any cost?
There are tyrannical Arabian parents, too, that,
deaf to the voice of conscience, disregard their
offspring's future welfare; but over there one
cannot look upon it as an abuse of authority if
the parents make the choice. The seclusion of
the women renders such a course imperative.
Living altogether apart from the male world,
they communicate only with their nearest relatives
of the sterner sex, though one must admit that

MEMBERS OF AN ARABIAN HAREM

despite all precautions an acquaintance is now and then formed and continued. However, according to the predominating rule no girl ever sees her intended except perhaps from a window, or speaks to him until the evening of the nuptials.

Meanwhile he does not remain a complete stranger to her, since his mother and sisters and aunts vie with one another in describing him in minute detail. Sometimes the pair have played together as children, boys and girls being permitted unrestricted companionship to the age of nine, and a few years later the youth asks the father of his erstwhile playmate for her hand, but not without having sounded the prospective wife through his mother or sister. Whenever a young man brings his suit forward, the careful sire commences by asking: "How did you manage to see my daughter," which enquiry is properly answered with: "I have never had the privilege of setting eyes upon your esteemed daughter, but I know all of her virtues and graces from my relatives."

Only in the event of the suitor being quite unsatisfactory does he meet with prompt rejection at the hands of the father, who usually requests time to consider the offer. This parent then comports himself at home as if nothing had happened, observing wife and daughter narrowly in conversation with them. Casually he lets the remark slip that he is thinking of giving a gentleman's party soon, and when asked whom he intends to

invite enumerates his friends. If he notices any
sign of pleasure at mention of the suitor's name
he becomes convinced that the women on both
sides are agreed. He thereupon states to his
daughter that So-and-So has applied for her, and
he inquires what her views may be. Her answer
usually settles the question; none but a heartless
or domineering father will decide without waiting
for her consent or refusal.

In this respect our progenitor showed his never
failing justice by leaving his children to determine
their own fate. My sister Zuena was but twelve
when a distant cousin presented himself. The
Sultan, although annoyed because of her youth-
fulness, would not refuse the young man point
blank without consulting her. Zuena had just
lost her mother, so, having no one to advise her,
for the sheer fun of the thing she accepted her
cousin, and the Sultan assented.

Cases arise in which betrothal, and even espousal,
takes place at a very young age. Two brothers
of Zanzibar had engaged to unite their progeny,
and when the boy, on one side, was seventeen or
eighteen, and the girl, on the other, about seven
or eight, talk already began on the subject of
carrying the match into effect. The boy's mother,
a prudent, clear-sighted woman, complained to
me of her husband's and his brother's obstinacy
in attempting to force upon her a daughter-in-
law who was little more than an infant, and whom

she would have to take care of and bring up. As for the girl's mother, she was inconsolable over the loss threatening her. Between them, the female parents contrived to obtain a postponement of two years. What eventually came of the affair, I am unable to say, for I left the island.

A betrothal is formally announced to friends and acquaintances by servants, who go from house to house, dressed in their best, distributing invitations to the wedding, and being presented with gratuities by those called upon. Great activity now develops at the bride's home, since the nuptials may occur in a month's time, at all events the period of betrothal is never a long one, nor is much preparation necessary in the favoured South. Orientals have no conception of the countless articles indispensable to the European; an Arabian "fiancée" would be struck dumb at the sight of a European "trousseau." Why are people here so fond of loading themselves with ballast? But the Arabian bride gets relatively little for her dowry, which may consist—according to her position—of handsome clothes, jewellery, slaves of both sexes, houses, plantations, and cash. Not only her parents, but the groom and his parents bestow gifts upon her, all of which remain her personal property.

During the first week a wife of high station is expected to change her clothes two or three times a day. A special bridal dress, like the white gown and tulle veil, is not in vogue; but the lady must wear new things, from top to toe, the choice being left to her, and sometimes resulting in the gayest assortment of colours, which however do not offend the eye. Then certain perfumes are made for the occasion—*riha*, for instance, a costly hair ointment composed of powdered sandal-wood, musk, saffron, and attar of roses. Aloes-wood, musk, and amber combined form an agree-able incense. Baking, confectionery and securing animals to be slaughtered busy a number of people also.

A tiresome usage the woman must submit to is spending her final week of maidenhood in a dark room, when she abstains from wearing any but the plainest garments—on the supposition that she will look all the more beautiful at the auspicious hour. During the weeks preceding it she is beset by visitors. All the old women she has ever known, particularly her nurses, whom she may not have seen for years, pay their respects with open palm. The chief eunuch, too, that once shaved her hair proudly reminds her how he performed the eminent service, begs her con-tinued patronage—and a keepsake. Usually he receives a valuable shawl, a ring for the little finger of his left hand, a watch, or a few gold pieces.

The husband-to-be, though spared confinement to a dark room, is not exempt from rewarding anybody who has ever done a single thing for the lady or himself. He remains at home the last three days, and is only visible to his most intimate friends, meanwhile exchanging compliments and presents with his adored one through their families.

The marriage rite is generally enacted after sunset, and not in a mosque but at the bride's house, by a cadi, or, if none is available, by a man of acknowledged piety. The principal performer, so to speak, does not come upon the scene at all, her father, brother, or some other close male relative representing her. Should she be without male connections, she appears personally before the cadi, muffled up beyond recognition, and repeats the usual set phrases in a tone of voice almost inaudible; the room must be empty when she enters it, cadi, groom, and witnesses following in and going away after her. Upon the ceremony's conclusion the newly wedded retires to her apartments, while the husband and the rest of the men hold a feast.

Official surrender of the wife does not always figure as an immediate sequel to the tying of the knot, being customarily adjourned until the third day. Beautified and adorned to the utmost, she is taken to her new home, about nine or ten o'clock at night, by her female relations, where she is met by the husband and his male connections. If she bears the higher rank of the two, she remains seated when he comes in. She waits for him to address her, upon which she may speak to him. But she still keeps her face concealed; before she unveils, the husband must signify his devotion in the shape of a gift corresponding to his resources. Poor men bestow a few pence, but the rich hand over large sums.

On this night the master of the establishment opens it up for universal hospitality, lasting as long as two weeks. Friends, acquaintances, even strangers are welcome, and can eat and drink to their hearts' content. True, neither wine nor beer is proffered, and the Abadites (the sect we belong to) are forbidden to smoke tobacco; nevertheless, people enjoy themselves thoroughly. They eat what they please, drink milk of almonds and lemonade, sing, execute war dances, and listen to recitations. Eunuchs burn incense the while, and sprinkle rose-water on the guests.

Honeymoon journeys are unknown in the East. The young couple keep strictly at home the first week or two, and see nobody, after the lapse of which term the wife receives her female friends, who come in throngs every evening to offer their congratulations.

CHAPTER XIII

SOCIAL CUSTOMS

CALLS MADE IN THE EVENING—WITH ESCORT OF
ARMED SLAVES—FORM OF RECEPTION BY THE
HOSTESS—ETIQUETTE CONCERNING SLIPPERS
—CONVERSATION—RIGID EXCLUSION OF MEN
FROM ASSEMBLIES OF WOMEN—SAYING GOOD-
BYE—ROYAL AUDIENCES—ORDER OF PROCEED-
INGS THEREAT—OBLIGATION TO ATTEND THEM
—VISITS BETWEEN MEN.

ANY lady who wanted to pay a call was supposed
to have her coming heralded by a servant; we
rarely took the liberty of making impromptu
visits. Residents of the town we went to see on
foot, but into the country we would ride on mule
or horse back. In Zanzibar you dress up for these
occasions, just as you do in Germany, for the
purpose of honouring your hostess and exhibiting
your finery (which you hope will throw other
people's into the shade).

Mahometan ladies avoid showing themselves
in public during the daytime; custom bids them
give preference to early morning or to nightfall.
Zanzibar had no street lighting when I lived there,
so that we had to provide our own means of
illumination. We employed large lanterns, some

no less than four or five feet round. The handsomest resembled Russian churches: a big central cupola and four smaller ones. In each division burned a candle, whose rays glowed through a coloured glass. The wealthy would take several of these lanterns, which were borne by strong servants, middle class people doing with one.

You have an escort of armed slaves, but they look more formidable than they really are. They used to give us a lot of trouble, and to cause great expense. For all their weapons, with the exception of rifles and revolvers, were inlaid with gold or silver, and these rascals would put them in pledge for a trifle with some East Indian usurer, simply to quench their thirst in *pomba* (palm wine). So what could a mistress do but buy the articles back at ten times the amount, or fit the creatures out anew after having them soundly whipped? I am sorry to say, however, that even this severe deterrent was not as effective as it ought to have been.

Thus a lady would start out with a dozen or more armed slaves, by twos preceding her and her lantern bearers, a number of highly bedizened waiting women bringing up the rear. If a pedestrian were met, whatever his rank, the slaves motioned him out of the road, and he had to step into a side street, or shop, or doorway, until the procession had gone by. Only it was found difficult to enforce this rule, excepting in the case

Photograph by A. C. Gomes & Co., Zanzibar

IN ZANZIBAR'S COMMERCIAL QUARTER

of the royal family; other ladies of distinction were not always able to assert their rights, since the roughs and rowdies objected to that form of deference. Although propriety everywhere ordains the quietest and most unobtrusive behaviour outdoors, nature was not to be denied, and the procession wound gaily along with such loud talking and joking that the inquisitive flocked to their windows or doors, or out upon their flat roofs.

Arrived at your destination, you sent in your name. But there was no tiresome twiddling of thumbs in a dark hallway or ante-chamber while the lady of the house was putting the last touches to her toilette. You followed close upon the announcer's heels, and were received in the hostess's room, or, if the moon was up, on the roof—kept scrupulously clean, and edged by a balustrade. The hostess sits on a long, richly embroidered cushion, or divan, three or four inches thick, her back supported by another (against the wall). She does not come to meet one, as in the West real or pretended cordiality would bid her, but rises in token of personal regard for the visitor or of respect for higher rank.

Toward strangers of all classes an Arabian woman is very reticent and reserved, though between dear friends differences of birth and position count for nothing. I admit the Southerner to be terribly jealous, but look how much more passionately she loves than the cold

Northerner! Down there the heart is lord supreme;
here frosty reason too often holds complete sway,
but perhaps one should accept the harder life as
justification therefor.

After kissing the hostess on the head, the hand,
or the border of her shawl—persons equal in rank
clasp hands—one sits down on the divan but, if
one happens to be her inferior in station, not
without her request, which signified, one acknowledges her dignity by sitting a little way off.   The
veil is not discarded, nor anything but the foot-
gear.   The wooden sandals worn at home are
exchanged   for   handsomely   worked   leathern
slippers to go out in, these being lightly dropped
from the feet before entering a room, an obligation
from which absolutely no one is exempt.   It is
the business of the servants attending the door
to arrange the slippers carefully, so that their
owners may find them at once.   Here again a
canon of etiquette must be obeyed: the shoes of
the noblest in rank are placed in the middle, with
the others ranged about them in a semicircle.

Following upon the appearance of a guest, servants hand round coffee in tiny cups, each new
arrival bringing a repetition of coffee, supplemented
by fresh fruit and sweetmeats.   Pressing one to
take something would be thought barbarous.
Neither is the lady of the house obliged to keep the
conversation up to a set pitch—that painfully
artificial, European habit.   Instead, people chat

freely and spontaneously about any subject they like. Since there are no theatres, concerts, circuses, or balls to discuss, and one would rather omit profound reflections on the state of the weather, topics are limited. Usually the talk turns upon personal affairs and matters concerning agriculture. Everyone of substance in Zanzibar pursues agriculture, without much skill or system but with great enthusiasm. Conversation proceeds delightfully amid genial smiles and laughter unrestrained, for we Southerners enjoy a happy, mirthful disposition. And why not? The bright sunlight sheds unfailing cheer, and the lavishness of nature's voluntary gifts precludes all need of calculating for the morrow.

Under no circumstances may the master of the house venture into a room where his wife, mother, or sister is entertaining friends. Only the sovereign and his nearest male connections stand above this law. Hence, if one visits a married sister, her spouse must remain unseen till one departs. In the event of something important requiring to be communicated, he sends to beg her momentary presence in another room. Women do the same when their masculine relatives have friends with them. This regulation is enforced even when a lady has an all-day visitor, from six in the morning till seven at night, and then the men experience some difficulty in keeping out of the way. Of course the custom is

onerous, but the Oriental does not feel its pressure.
Brought up on certain views, and not knowing
any others to compare them with, he naturally
thinks they are quite right and proper. The
might of custom and its influence are much the
same everywhere. By no means would I deny
that the East has unnecessary or extravagant
usages, but is Europe free from such? There,
the strictest separation of the sexes; here, the
most unlicensed liberty of intercourse. In one
place, muffling up and close-veiling despite the
heat; in the other, low-necked dresses, the cold
climate notwithstanding. So you find extremes
and exaggeration wherever you go. That the
golden mean has not been discovered yet, is my
opinion.

Ladies' visits last three or four hours. Then
the slaves have to be wakened, and formed up to
resume the order of march. Meanwhile the
lanterns have been kept burning, a waste to be
sure, yet nevertheless fashionable. After giving
her guests a present, however small, the hostess
allows them to depart; they must be back at
midnight, the latest term for the fifth prayer.
One great advantage accrues to Arabian women;
they are not obliged to express thanks for their
entertainment after a party or a visit—a decided
improvement on paying your hostess the prettiest
compliments to her face, and vilifying her as soon
as you are outside the door.

An old custom in Zanzibar demands that the ruler of the land grant interviews twice a day—before breakfast and after the fourth prayer—to the males of his family, his ministers, his other officials, and everybody who may desire to speak to him. The hall of audience, or *barza*, was situated on the ground floor in our palace, close to the sea and commanding a beautiful view over its animated surface. Though very large, this hall was sometimes inadequate for the crowd assembled. Like every Arabian apartment, it was fitted out with striking simplicity, containing nothing but carpets, mirrors up to the ceiling, clocks, and chairs at the sides. Since no Arab of eminence goes out alone, a couple of hundred satellites were always swarming about the entrance; who could find room sat on the stone benches running along the walls, the rest waiting in the open square in front of the house for their masters or friends. The gentlemen invariably came to audiences in full state costume—turban, *djocha* (an outer coat reaching to the ankles), and sash.

At home an Arab wears on his head—shorn bare once a week—a white cap often prettily embroidered; to go out he puts on his turban. It takes some skill to build this up artistically, and some time, for which reason a man removes the delicate structure with infinite precaution. The cloth used for turbans is relatively cheap, but the material for a sash may run up to two hundred silver dollars. A noble always owns a lot of sashes, and changes them as a man does his neckties here. Plain white or black silk girdles are worn by the less prosperous, by the elderly, and by those indifferent to fashion. An Arab's costume, as I have mentioned, is incomplete without his weapons.

Before a man of note enters the audience hall he takes off his shoes just as he arrives at the door; a plebeian, at some distance from it. In this there is no suspicion of despotism; it is an ancient custom, to which everyone willingly subscribes. To all ranks the Arab pays due honour and respect; especially does he feel sentiments of instinctive reverential devotion toward the royal family.

When the *barza* is full the Sultan starts. In my father's lifetime the procession would move as follows: First a company of Negro guards, then the junior eunuchs, the senior eunuchs, the Sultan, the Sultan's elder sons, and finally his younger sons. At the door of the hall guards and eunuchs formed a lane, through which my father and brothers entered the *barza*. All present rose to greet Seyyid Saïd, his departure taking place in the same order again. If a noble left before he did, he would perhaps walk down the room with him a few steps, while the others stood up for that moment.

Coffee was rarely served at the morning, but regularly at the evening audiences. Petitions and complaints were presented and answered by word of mouth, documentary transaction of business being unfavoured. Usually, therefore, petitioners had to come in person. Matters of minor importance were handed over to a minister, cadi, or head eunuch. An audience lasted two hours or so, and questions unattended to were relegated to the next day.

Princes of the blood visit the assembly dating from about their fifteenth year, when they are bound to do so. Each notable, likewise, must appear once a day before his sovereign, unless prevented by the most urgent circumstances. In case of prolonged absence, the Sultan sends an inquiry, going himself if illness is reported. No disease, however virulently contagious, neither cholera nor smallpox, acts as a deterrent. For everything is in the hand of God.

Gentlemen make calls upon one another at the same hour as the ladies, that is to say after seven at night by preference. An Arab must have a definite object in going out. He knows not the existence of the "constitutional," and if he sees a European pacing his roof in the evening imagines this some form of Christian prayer. I need give no particulars about visits between gentlemen in Zanzibar, which very nearly resemble those of the opposite sex. The conversation embraces a larger field of topics, both local and national; the last audience is discussed, the various petitions brought forward there, the lawsuits settled. Europeans being admitted to the audiences and to male social gatherings, they are more familiar with that side of our patriarchal doings than with the secluded life of the Eastern women.

CHAPTER XIV

MAHOMETAN FESTIVALS

THE MONTH OF RAMADAN—DAILY FASTING—
NOCTURNAL FEASTING AND HOSPITALITY
—PRESENTATION OF HOLIDAY GIFTS—WATCH-
ING FOR THE NEW MOON—GENERAL REJOICINGS
—THE BANYANS—HENNA, AND THE WAY TO
USE IT—PUBLIC PRAYERS—THE "GREAT
FEAST"—PILGRIMAGES TO MECCA—A TENTH
TO THE POOR—HOW PAUPERISM IS CONSE-
QUENTLY A NECESSARY INSTITUTION.

IT is no doubt well known that the Mahometan
world celebrates a month of the year by fasting
throughout the whole of each day, an observance
not to be compared with the Catholic, which is
far easier. This fasting is compulsory for all
adherents of Islam, the children over twelve
included. My mother being a woman of extraordinary piety, she made me keep the month of
Ramadan when I was nine. Surely it is a great
hardship for a child of nine to abstain entirely
from food and drink during a period lasting
fourteen hours and a half. But hunger is much less
unbearable than the raging thirst one experiences
in the tropics. At my age I naturally had rather
faint ideas about religion, and I confess, to my

shame, that I occasionally stole a sip of water;
on being closely questioned by my mother, I
repentantly acknowledged the transgression, when
I was forgiven upon the understanding that I
would not break the sacred law again. Strict
obedience to the rules would not even allow one
to swallow one's spittle purposely.

At four o'clock in the morning a cannon shot is
fired off as a signal for the fasting to begin. Were
one in the middle of eating, one would stop immediately; if one were just about to raise a vessel
with fluid to one's mouth, one would desist at
hearing the cannon's report. From that moment
no adult in good health may eat a morsel or drink
a drop. There is a general preference for sleeping
during the day in the month of Ramadan, and
for enjoying oneself until late at night. The
sun goes down at six, so that after prayers the
fast may be broken at half-past six. Fruit and
cold spring-water in earthenware jars are held
in readiness as first refreshment of the sufferer.
Soon the family gathers to consume an Epicurean
meal, by way of compensation. A simple, frugal
liver, the Arab yet develops into a glutton at his
repasts in Ramadan.

The evenings, or rather nights, are spent together sociably, with religious hymns, recitations,
stories, interspersed by eating and drinking. At
midnight a cannon wakes up sleepers and bids
them prepare the *suhur*, a meal served between

BRITISH SAILORS PLAYING CRICKET AT ZANZIBAR

three and four o'clock in one's private room. The whole month passes in this manner. At first there are cases of fainting fits, and people grow visibly thin. By degrees they become accustomed to the deprivation; fewer sleep all day, and many who came out only for prayers and the meal at half-past six show themselves in public as usual.

All members of every household must strictly keep the fast, and one is expected to admonish one's servants. Plantation labourers, being usually without a religion, are at liberty to fast or not, as they please. Young children and invalids are excused, as I said, but the latter must make up the fasting after recovery. Travellers and women in a state of confinement are also exempted, though for them likewise the duty is purely deferred.

Fasting is of course no mere outer observance; in Ramadan the faithful Moslem submits to rigid self-examination, that he may discover his moral faults and sue forgiveness of his sins—just as in Holy Week the devout Christian prepares for the sacrament. One tries to do all the good one can this month, even avoiding to kill wild beasts. Hence the celebration of Ramadan tends to soften the heart, to bring man nearer to God, to improve and elevate him for the time being, if not for his whole life.

The Arabs' traditional hospitality now reaches its height, in fact becomes a religious tenet. Everyone who has a house or family entertains at his board a huge number of people, some of whom he does not so much as know by name. He simply asks the prayer-reader at the mosque he attends to send a certain number of people to supper every night. Nor are his guests restricted to the poor and humble, but frequently include men of great substance, strangers away from home at this sacred period of the year. To provide for such a one always delights the truly hospitable Arab. Nobody demurs at accepting food and drink from an inferior; least of all would payment be thought of, since an offer of money would constitute an insult. Under principles like these selfishness cannot take deep root, and happy the nation that regards brotherly love as an inviolable duty.

To some extent Ramadan resemble the weeks preceding Christmas, since gifts are distributed at the beginning of the next month. Needlework is not often presented, and never excepting to intimates. The difficulties incident to secrecy are those familiar here; many a time have I seen a solitary figure bending over her task in an unfrequented nook by the bright light of the African moon. Generally, presents are bought ready-made, and the jewellers do the best business. This trade is entirely absorbed by East Indian Banyans, unsurpassed at cunning, deception, and trickery. Highly expert in their handicraft, they have altogether superseded the Arabian gold-

smith. Orders pour in upon them at this season,
and they refuse none. Did we want to insure the
prompt making up of an article commissioned, we
would send a couple of armed slaves to watch our
man at his job, and to prevent his executing
other orders. A drastic method, no doubt, but
one (invented by a sister of mine) absolutely
necessary with these wretched Hindu blacklegs,
whose word counts for nothing, and who are
miserable cowards into the bargain.

Jewellery and arms form the favourite objects
for donation, though anything else is acceptable,
blood horses, white mules, and—horrible to the
civilised European—even slaves!

Thus the last week is full of activity and expectation. The night of the twenty-sixth of
Ramadan is particularly sacred, as Mahomet then
received the Koran from Heaven. When, at last,
the great day dawns, or rather when dusk sets
in, the whole population has no thought but to
descry the new moon. Our almanacs are only
intended for scholars, and would be of no avail as
the new moon must be actually visible before the
fasting can end. Whoever owns a telescope or
opera-glass is greatly envied, the coveted instru-
ment travelling from hand to hand; friends and
acquaintances send from a distance to borrow it.
Our father would despatch men with sharp eyes
to the roof of the fort—a relic of the Portuguese
dominion—and to the mastheads of his ships,

with the mission of spying out the silver crescent. At eventide universal suspense prevails; each moment someone imagines he has heard the happy longed-for signal—every sound is mistaken for it. Finally, when the shot booms out, the whole town gives vent to loud jubilation and exchanges of festive compliments.

In the country the matter is less simple. There the ruler's forethought can guarantee no oral token that the right time has come. People residing on plantations send a mounted messenger into town, who after the big gun's report may ride back with the certain news that the moon has actually been seen. Others let slaves climb up the highest palm trees, whence they scan the horizon. Now and then the sentinel mistakes a light little strip of cloud for the lunar sickle; the fast is broken prematurely, and the error remains undiscovered until tidings arrive from town. That means making up by renewed abstinence— a severe shock to the holiday spirit.

During the last week there is not only a great amount of baking, but quantities of oxen, sheep, goats, gazelles, chickens, and pigeons are purchased, overflowing the stables. We do not eat veal, and Moslems are strictly prohibited from partaking of pork. People in easy circumstances have money given out to the poor so that they too may satisfy their needs.

Upon the sound of the cannon, allowing the

actual initiation of the so-called "Little Feast," an Arabian house becomes the scene of ever-increasing excitement and tumult. Hundreds of radiant mortals hasten hither and thither, forgetting their usual dignified deportment, all intent on pronouncing blessings and good wishes to family and friends. Amid these feelings of religious exaltation two enemies are apt to clasp hands in mutual pardon, hoping to have earned God's by their own previous purification of heart.

Owing to the lively rejoicings, the manifold exclaimings in sundry tongues, the cursings at overworked slaves, sleep is almost impossible that night. Servants especially find rest out of the question. The butchers pounce upon their bellowing or squeaking prey in order to kill them, having first uttered the prescribed formula "In the name of God the All-Merciful!" And in accord with holy ritual the beast's throat is slit, its head chopped off, and its carcass skinned. So it reaches the kitchen in time to be done for the morrow's banquet.

Our yard looked like an ocean of gore after the wholesale slaughtering. The vegetarians living in Zanzibar, the Banyans, hated our feasts, and shunned the places where animals were put to the knife. They are virtually the only manufacturers in the island, and at the same time the most usurious skinflints. Bitterly loathed by their victims, they are mocked by them on these occasions in cruel fashion.

Pretending that some rich lady wishes to make a purchase, rough people lure the Banyans—ever on the lookout for trade—into the shambles, there holding them up to general derision. At all events these star-worshippers, however corrupt, faithfully obey the vegetarian teachings of their creed.

But it is not only the noise that keeps the ladies awake. They are racking their brains how to outshine one another in the splendours of dress. The festival endures three days, upon each of which a new outfit of clothes must be worn— entirely new to the smallest detail, from head to foot. Perfumes are then employed in such profusion as to suggest for analogy the quantities of beer consumed in Berlin at Whitsuntide. Many an Arabian lady spends five hundred silver dollars a year on scents, and their odour would probably overpower one but for the windows and doors being constantly open.

An important part in the oriental gala toilette is played by henna, derived from the leaves of a shrub, and used to colour the hands of women and children to a lasting red, though also to cure pimples, freckles, and itching. Still, henna leaves —they resemble those of the myrtle—are not efficacious alone; after drying and pulverisation they are mixed with lemon juice and a little water, then kneaded into a dough, which is set out in the sun, and finally treated again with lemon juice to prevent hardening.

The recipient lies rigid at full length on her back. First the dough is applied to the feet; their surface remains untouched, but each toe is covered, and the soles and sides. Next a layer of soft leaves is put on, and tightly bandaged down. Then the hands are proceeded with in the same manner exactly. The back of the hand is left free, the edge of the palm and each finger to the first joint being plastered with dough and en-swathed. Motionless does the vain beauty lie on her bed all night, that she be not disfigured through the shifting of the dough. For, mark, only the parts I have specified may be tinted; if henna should appear on the back of the hand, or above the first finger joint, that would be thought hideous. No defence is possible against mosquitoes and flies, though the wealthy can have them fanned away by slaves until morning, when the dough is carefully removed. That night the torture begins anew, and the following night once more, since three applications are necessary to produce a rich, dark red, which will keep a month, despite all washing. Elderly ladies and children do not submit to this operation, but use henna, in a liquefied form, as a cooling ablution for the skin of their hands.

On the morning of the festal day everybody is up at four o'clock, and tarries long over the first prayer, earnestly thanking the Omnipotent Creator and Director of the Universe for all blessings vouch-

safed, and for the ills inflicted with the purpose of
trying us. These orisons concluded, bedizened
ladies are seen hurrying along the veranda; they
intend exhibiting their finery to a few others, as
an hour later, amid the general splendour and
magnificence, an individual has no chance to
distinguish herself. One might think of a comparison with a ballroom, were not the pallid monotony of white so conspicuous in the North. With
us, in the East, only bright assortments of colour
are approved. How a European fashionable would
be shocked at an Arabian woman, dressed in her
long, red silk, shirt-like garments, patterned and
corded all over with gold and silver thread, and
wearing a pair of green satin trousers! Of course
she would find it extraordinary, just as I did when
I first saw Europeans going about in grey with
grey and black with black. I disliked the colours
of civilisation, and was some time persuading myself to adopt "elegant" tastes.

At six o'clock another cannon. Then report
after report to celebrate the event. Foreign men-
of-war chancing to be in the harbour join the firing
by salutes of twenty-one guns. Every Arab who
can manifests his joy by shooting, and he spares
no powder; a stranger would certainly believe
the town under bombardment. All ships are
gaily decorated; flags fly from yardarms and
masts of native and alien vessels alike.

An hour more, and all the mosques fill up,

hundreds of people unable to get admission performing their devotions outside them. The exercise of Mussulman worship entails bodily effort, as the worshipper must repeatedly bend low down, touching his forehead to the ground in the Divine presence. In a dirty, stony street this is no trifle. But no loyal disciple of Islam will allow rain, storm, or anything else to interfere with his prayers, and upon feast days he regards it as a serious duty to offer them within or close to a mosque. Seyyid Saïd was wont to obey the rule, visiting a holy edifice nearby with his sons and an innumerable escort. Another salvo of artillery denotes the conclusion of the religious service, and from that moment one may revel to the heart's content in one's favourite gastronomic delicacies, the fast actually ceasing after the early prostrations.

We women awaited the Sultan's return in his apartment, all rising as he entered, to step forward and congratulate him, and to imprint a respectful kiss on his hand. An aristocratic hand of either sex has a good deal to go through on a religious holiday; it is washed and perfumed without end, from dawn to dusk. Equals kiss each other on the hand; middle-class persons touch a superior's inclined head with the lips; a common woman may only salute the feet.

At these festivals my father would order a grand distribution of presents, which were similar

to those described in a former chapter, and whose
handing over was effected under supervision of
the chief eunuch. But this time gifts were
universal. The Sultan donated not to his family
alone, but to Asiatic or African nobles sojourning
at the capital, to all civil functionaries, soldiers
and their officers, sailors and their captains, the
stewards of his forty-five plantations, and to all
his slaves, perhaps counting about eight thousand.
The charming German custom of children giving
birthday and Christmas presents to their parents
is not in vogue in my country, where one's birthday passes unobserved, and where the head of
the family never receives anything from his
children.

Mahometans keep but two festivals a year,
which might seem incomprehensible to Catholics,
with their frequent holidays. Two months lie
between the "Little Feast" and the "Great
Feast," either being known as Bairam. The
second forms a virtual repetition of the other,
yet is celebrated more gorgeously, and hearts are
keyed to a still higher pitch of sacred fervour. It
is the season, too, for the grand pilgrimage to
Mecca, undertaken at least once in the life of all
true believers able to go. Undismayed by cholera
and other diseases that carry off thousands of
pilgrims, zealous Islamites repair in untold numbers to the Prophet's holy city, there suing pardon
for their sins. The needy must travel huge

PILGRIMS SURROUNDING THE PULPIT AND KAABA (SACRED SHRINE) AT MECCA

distances on foot, and the voyages on shipboard, where they almost lie on the top of one another, are appalling. But on they journey; their fate is in the hand of the Lord. Truly such steadfastness, fearing no exertions, no hardships, no dangers, deserves a favourable eye.

The "Great Feast" falls on the tenth day of the twelfth month, and lasts from three to seven days. Everyone in a position to afford buying a sheep has one killed on the first day, and delivered to the poor. The law prescribes that the animal must be perfect, without a single flaw, deficient by not so much as a tooth. Neither the owner of the sacrificial beast, nor his family, nor even his servants may touch its flesh; every morsel belongs to the indigent.

In the real Oriental countries (I except Turkey, Egypt, and Tunis because of their half-European civilisation) no one understands the meaning of "stocks" and "bonds," so that the word "investment" does not exist. Property comprises plantations, houses. slaves, cattle, jewellery, and cash, and his creed bids the Moslem surrender to the poor a tenth of all that remains to him from his crops, the rental of his houses, or other sources of revenue. Furthermore, his treasures in gold, silver, and precious stones must be appraised by an expert, and of the bulk one-tenth set aside for the poor—income tax and property tax in one! And this is all done without regulation by the authorities, everybody being bound by his own soul. But it is a law of the Prophet strictly obeyed, and carried out *sans* comment or discussion, on the principle of not allowing the left hand to know what the right is doing. And one complies with the most scrupulous exactness so as not to be tormented by remorse or pangs of conscience.

Under such circumstances every Mahometan state must, of necessity almost, contain an army of paupers as an institution. How else could the duty of self-taxation be absolved? Now, these paupers resemble not the unfortunate creatures seen here, but half perhaps own more than they actually want. Begging is their profession, it is their second nature, and if they stopped they would be unhappy. Sometimes begging passes down as an inherited vocation, when one may be addressed: "Do you not know me? I am the son (or daughter, or sister-in-law, etc.) of So and-So, to whom you were so liberal when he (or she) was alive. I have taken his (or her) place, therefore if you have anything to give please send it to me."

Whenever we had to fulfil vows, which happened several times a year, these paupers would flock by to share in the customary dispensing of alms. Or if anyone was sick they would get wind of the fact, and would stand guard under the windows in reliefs, earning handsome remuneration for doing so. Whether this form of charity is brotherly love, or intended as a means of propitiating the Almighty, I cannot say; anyhow, the custom is a beautiful one.

Many beggars, however, are a mass of sores and ulcers. Some go about with their noses rotted away or other dreadful mutilation; they are victims to a disease we call *belas*, hands and feet turning white as snow. Nobody will have aught to do with these people, whose ailment is accounted contagious. I do not know if the malady in question is leprosy. But the unhappy wretches get plentiful alms, which render their piteous existence a little more bearable. Not that all the giving stops at the great Bairam feast. Those who have been ill, or otherwise detained, through a journey perhaps, from attending the distribution, never dream of relinquishing their claim. Weeks, months, may have sped by since the festival, even the next may be approaching; they none the less come, and ask for their presents.

CHAPTER XV

Medical Treatment

CUPPING—KNEADING—SWALLOWING SENTENCES
FROM THE KORAN—CONSULTATION OF FOREIGN
PHYSICIANS—MALTREATMENT BY DOMESTIC
REMEDIES—SUPERSTITIOUS PRACTICES—POS-
SESSION BY SPIRITS, GOOD AND EVIL—EXORCISM
AND PROPITIATION—FEMALE DOCTORS NEEDED
IN ZANZIBAR.

PEOPLE grow up in Eastern lands without particular attention to any rules or care of health.
Only severe illness calls forth aid to nature, but
the means employed are pure hocus-pocus. The
grand, universal remedy is cupping, for every
ailment, from smallpox to cholera, this atrocious
operation being also regarded as a preventive.
Hence persons in robust condition submit themselves to cupping at least once a year, that their
blood may be cleansed, and their bodies strength-
ened against possible future sickness. I remember bursting into loud screams on a certain occasion at Bet il Mtoni, when I saw a sister of mine
stark and white after blood-letting; she had
fainted away from the weakness caused by the
loss, and I supposed her dead.

Kneading of the limbs is agreeable and

beneficial. Our slaves were highly expert thereat; I
mentioned before how they sent us to sleep and
woke us up by this process. It is much in vogue
for various kinds of indisposition, especially "pains
in the body." Vomiting—another favourite cure
—demands the administration of nauseous herbs,
concocted to make a brew so horrible that its
mere approach to one's nose produces the desired
effect.

In case of a grave malady, we appeal to the
Higher Power, using sentences from the Koran.
Some individual of known exemplary life writes
the sentences on a plate with a solution of saffron.
Mixed with rosewater, this writing turns into a
beverage for the patient, who takes three doses a
day. The greatest caution is observed lest a drop
of the sacred drink be spilled. I have myself
taken this medicine for several weeks at a stretch
while down with a malignant fever.

Exceptional instances occurred when a medical
man—either a real doctor or a magician—would
be summoned to an invalid's bedside. My sister
Chole, after protracted suffering from an obstinate,
unceasing earache, was to see a noted Persian
doctor, and I got permission to attend the consultation. Chole was wrapped up so that she
could not be recognised, with however the ailing
ear left uncovered. Then she seated herself on
a divan. On her right my father assumed his
position, standing, and my brother Khaled on her

left. My younger brothers, dressed in state raiment and fully armed, formed a semicircle about them. Escorted by a band of eunuchs the physician came into the room, other eunuchs having been stationed in sundry parts of the house to warn away female inmates who might otherwise have met the Persian. He, of course, dared not himself address my sister, but carried on his examination through my father and brothers.

When, at a later date, I was afflicted with typhoid, and all native remedies had failed, my father's sister Assha decided to call in a European. My father having died, and I being to some extent my own mistress, the ceremonious visitation of Chole was not repeated. The doctor in question, though familiar with Arabian customs, insisted on feeling my pulse, to which my aunt, who was sincerely anxious about me, at last gave her sanction. Still, a host of eunuchs were marshalled, and, like Chole, I had to be enswathed beyond recognition (I was unconscious at the time, and heard the story from Assha afterward). Upon the mediciner asking to see my tongue, the chief eunuch berated him so violently because of this impudent request, that the disciple of Esculapius left the place, feeling grossly insulted in his professional dignity.

The Arab has no idea of classifying diseases. He knows but two kinds, "pains in the body" and "pains in the head." To the first category belong any complaints affecting stomach, liver, or kidneys, while under the second he lists all manifestations of distress assailing the head, whether sunstroke or softening of the brain. No one ever discovers the fundamental cause of an illness, and if domestic nostrums prove unavailing, sometimes a European doctor will be sent to for medicine. But he is in an awkward predicament —forbidden to see the patient, and uncertainly informed concerning her case. Small wonder, then, if he return the wrong medicine, or, at best, something innocuous.

Dieting is likewise unheard of. The victim to cholera, smallpox, or typhoid showing an appetite, he may gratify it with any eatables the kitchen affords. What one's nature craves must be good for one, is the supposition. Thus Divine ordinance rules in everything, and usually forsooth, blinds the Moslem to the danger of contagion. No one would dream, for instance, of segregating sufferers from the smallpox. The bath-house I mentioned, above which went the passage connecting Bet il Sahel and Bet il Tani, fell to ruin, and served as a refuse pit. Nevertheless, when the clamour for additional quarters grew, new ones were built upon the decayed wreck, so that the inhabitants virtually lived over a mass of filth.

Unhappily, smallpox ravages our island in regular recurrence, claiming thousands of victims.

The patient's whole body is smeared with a salve, and then exposed to the sun; or else cocoanut milk is applied. But when the patient is covered with sores, and he cannot endure the contact of the bedclothes, he is laid on a soft straw mat or a large fresh banana leaf whose stiff spine has been removed. No method of internal relief is attempted, and water is not allowed to touch him.

Consumption, unfortunately no rare guest, either receives no treatment whatever, although the disease most feared, and held to be infectious— as the European medical fraternity believes. A consumptive is shunned by everyone; people avoid shaking hands with him, and will not drink out of a glass he has used. Not a few of my own family succumbed to phthisis in their very prime. Things belonging to the dead were disinfected; clothes and bedding were washed by the seashore, and gold and silver articles made red-hot.

Whooping-cough among children appears as often as in Germany, They drink dew gathered from banana leaves, and superstition does the rest; the dried rind of a pumpkin is cut up into small discs, these strung together, and suspended round the neck. Boils of a certain kind are overlaid with shrivelled onion skins, taking the place of court plaster. If you want a boil to burst you administer warm dough. Never a doctor! Nothing but primitive domestic remedies!

On the other ·hand, soothsayers are greatly in demand, and well paid.   We usually consulted an old one-eyed hag of fifty.   Her magic outfit was contained in a dirty leather bag: little shells and pebbles, bleached bones of animals, bits of broken glass and china, rusty iron nails, mutilated copper and silver coins, etc.   When you ordered her to answer a question, she would pray to God for guidance, shake up the bag, and spill out the whole mess in front of her.   According to the position of all that rubbish she would then prophesy as to the patient's recovery.   Chance seemed to favour this woman, since her prognostications often came true which rendered the business doubly lucrative, each successful forecast bringing an additional gratuity.

External injuries are of course more easily got rid of; tinder, for example, will stop a wound from bleeding.   But with fractures it is a different matter, as I learned to my cost.   I was quite young, and therefore ineligible to sit at meals.   The Sultan one day sent me some delicacies on a plate which I was in such a hurry to exhibit to my mother that I tumbled downstairs, and broke my forearm.   My aunt Assha and my brother Bargash bandaged it, but did not set the bones properly; hence it never became quite straight again, and it now constantly reminds me how sadly my countrymen need medical and surgical experts.

These pages of mine have thus far neglected a
highly important personage—his Satanic Majesty!
That nearly all Orientals believe in an actual
fiend is generally known, I imagine, though perhaps not that he is much given to taking up his
domicile within human beings. Hardly a child
in Zanzibar but what had been possessed. So
soon as a new-born babe screams too vociferously,
or cannot be quieted, at once steps are taken to
drive out the devil. Tiny onions and garlic bulbs
arranged in a necklace for the child form the simple means of expulsion—not a bad idea if the
devil has a nose. Adults too are frequently
possessed, though far oftenest the women. The
outer signs are cramps, loss of appetite, listlessness,
a partiality for dark rooms, and like morbid
symptoms.

However, in order to find out if they are genuinely afflicted, a formal investigation takes
place. They or their relatives invite to the ceremony a company of individuals all reputed to be
possessed. The patient sits in a dark room,
with her head so wrapped up that not the faintest
glimmer of light could penetrate. She is fumigated
in the literal meaning of the word, for the censer
is held beneath her nasal organ under the cloth.
The company surround her, singing a peculiar
song, and occasionally wagging their heads. Nor
must a certain Abyssinian beverage be omitted,
prepared from wheat and dates brought just

within fermentation, and making a rather palatable drink.   Under these influences the heroine of the occasion goes into a sort of trance, and begins to talk incoherently.   At last she raves, stamps about, foams at the mouth.   She is now filled with the spirit.   The spectators address it, inquiring as to its intentions.   For not alone evil spirits but good spirits visit people, to comfort and protect them through life.   It may happen that a person is visited by a spirit of either kind simultaneously, when there is a furious battle, and none but the bravest dare stay for the terrifying conjurations and exorcisms.   An evil spirit may be expelled by a practiced seer, but with a good one you establish a compact: it must only at stated times visit its "protégée," by whom it will always be festally welcomed, and to whom it must reveal everything in store for herself or her family.

Connected with these idiotic superstitious habits are others that must be censured as brutal.   Many persons possessed will not allow the goats and hens chosen for their secret sacrificial rites to be slaughtered beforehand, but insist on drinking the blood warm.   Besides, they gobble uncooked meat, and raw eggs by the dozen.   No wonder if the poor wretches are laid up as a result.

The worst example is soonest followed.   Although Mahometans are greatly devoted to superstitions, the Omanites reject such nonsensical practices as I have been describing.   When they come to Africa, they at first think us barbarians, and would like to return immediately; however, they soon become receptive to the very notions they denounced, and adopt the most absurd. I was acquainted with an Arabian of that sort, who believed herself possessed by an evil spirit which made her ill; she was convinced that it could be propitiated if she held festivities in its honour.

It seems to me that it were better to send female physicians to Zanzibar than the demoralising brandy. Why must civilisation always be heralded by vice? Here is an opportunity for Christian brotherly love, and the difficulties would not be formidable. For my own part, I would willingly, if some association decided upon a suitable emissary, help her learn Arabic and Suahili—the least I could do for my beloved country. And the venture ought to be successful from a pecuniary point of view. But the doctor must be a woman. She could do more in the East than a dozen men—even here ladies often prefer female practitioners—and the hearts of Orientals are easily won by attentiveness, cheerfulness, and kindness.

CHAPTER XVI

SLAVERY

A RUINOUS RELEASE OF SLAVES—IDLENESS OF THE
NEGRO—A DEFENCE OF FLOGGING—SLAVES
AND CONCUBINES KEPT BY EUROPEANS IN
THE EAST—TO ABOLISH A TIME-HONOURED
CUSTOM, GO SLOW—MOSLEM "FANATICISM."

I WAS still a child when the term expired at the
end of which, according to a treaty between
England and Seyyid Saïd, slaveholding British
subjects living in Zanzibar were obliged to release
their slaves. It was a hard time for the owners,
who complained bitterly, and sent their wives
and daughters to enlist our sympathy, though of
course we could do nothing whatever for them.
Some kept a hundred or more slaves to work their
estates, which without labourers ceased to yield
revenues, and this meant ruin to the landlords.
Besides, our island now enjoyed the advantage
of being enriched by the presence of a few thousand loafers, tramps, and thieves. The grown-up
liberated infants understood freedom to signify
their exemption from work henceforth, and this
freedom they determined to make the most of,
whether they were entitled to shelter and substance from anyone, or not.

The humane anti-slavery apostles held aloof. Had they not attained their object in freeing those poor wretches from the degradation of serfdom? It was no concern of theirs what might happen afterward, and quite enough was done if their ladies knitted thick woollen stockings for those residents of the equatorial zone. Let the rulers down there deal with the lazy vagabonds as best they could. For everybody who has visited Africa, Brazil, North America, or any country where Negroes live, must be aware of their antipathy against work, whatever their virtues.

Only British subjects, I repeat, could hold no slaves after the date agreed upon; to my father England had no right to dictate concerning the government of his country, and therefore slavery still exists in Zanzibar, as it does in all Mahometan countries of the East. However, one must not form one's views on serfdom in the East by the precedents of North America and Brazil, since a Mahometan's slaves are infinitely better off.

A very bad feature is the trading. Taken from the interior, they have to make long marches to the coast, when they perish in shoals from hunger, thirst, and fatigue. But the slave-trader, exposed to the same hardships himself, can with no show of reason be branded a monster. His interest demands the slaves' preservation, as that caravan may represent his whole fortune. Their

AT THE MUNICIPAL FOUNTAIN

Photograph by A. C. Gomes & Co., Zanzibar

destination once reached, they are thoroughly well cared for. True, they must labour unpaid, but they are exempt from all anxiety, and assured of their maintenance, their masters desiring their welfare. Or is every non-Christian a heartless rascal?

Now, Negroes are very lazy, and will not work voluntarily, so they must be strictly watched. Neither are they perfect angels, for they include thieves, drunkards, runaways, incendiaries. What is to be done with these? To let them go unpunished would be out of the question, would mean to invite anarchy. And a creature of that class laughs at incarceration; he would feel immensely pleased at the prospect of resting a few days in a cool place, to gather strength for new misdeeds. Under such circumstances nothing remains but the lash. This gives rise to a great outcry in certain circles here, that always go upon abstract theory, and disdain studying a practical situation. Yes, flogging is inhuman; but let somebody provide a substitute. By the way, were it not better to administer an occasional whipping in German prisons, than to apply spurious "humanitarianism" indiscriminately to jailbirds of all feathers?

Tyranny must be condemned, whether inflicted upon the poor Negro, or the civilised white toiling in a Siberian mine. But to be fair you cannot ask the same standard of right and wrong

for every place. Slavery is a time-honoured
institution among Oriental peoples; that it will
ever be entirely abolished, I doubt; in any case,
attempts to destroy venerable custom at a single
dash are foolish.   Europeans should therefore
go slow, and, first of all themselves set us the right
example.   Numerous Europeans keep slaves in
the East, buying them to suit their convenience.
This is not reported at home, or is said to be done
"for the good of science."   An Arab using slaves
for field or housework, and a European compelling
them to the harder task of carrier, or "coolie"—
where's the difference from the moral standpoint?
Then, European slave owners do not invariably
set the negroes free after long service, as the Arabs
so often do, but resell them.

Considerable indignation once seized the Mahometans of Zanzibar upon learning how a departing Englishman had sold his black concubine—
not, to be sure, in the open market place (where an
English church now stands), but quietly to an
Arabian official.   Or another incident likewise
affronting our sense of propriety: A neighbour to
the French consul chastised his recalcitrant slave
as severely as he deserved, but, with a Negro's
usual cowardice and inability to bear pain in
silence, he struck up a frightful howl, which
brought down the French consul's rather arrogant
interference.   This gentleman was himself no
immaculate saint, seeming to hold the maxim,

Photograph by A. C. Gomes & Co., Zanzibar

WATER–CARRIERS PRACTISING THEIR VOCATION

"let others practice what I preach." For he lived with a negress he had bought, who had presented to him an excessively black little daughter—finally taken in by the French mission.

It should cause no surprise if upon such experiences the Arabs distrust Europeans, and if they long for the return of the days when they were safe from intrusive, subversive ideas. They believe that the abolition of slavery has the object of ruining them, and of thus upsetting Islamism. The English they particularly suspect as crafty schemers.

Should the real possibility exist of slavery's abrogation, one would have to proceed with the utmost slowness and care. The Negroes must be trained to think and to work, and their masters persuaded how the employment of improved agricultural machinery would enable them to do without hundreds of labourers now needed to cultivate their fields. The proprietor must be made to recognise that no one intends his ruin, and that justice is for him as well as for the serf. This would surely be more humane, more Christian, than ostentatiously building a church in the slave market, which was superfluous, by the way, because the two churches already standing, one Catholic, the other Protestant, had small congregations. Any such methods can only affront the Arab, who, like most other Orientals, is extremely conservative, and clings with the greatest tenacity to ancient traditions. He ought therefore not to have new ideas violently forced upon him which he finds incomprehensible and outrageous. Disagreement with European views brings upon him the immediate accusation of Moslem fanaticism, a thing vastly exaggerated, as was proved when I returned to Zanzibar after an absence of nineteen years. I had in the meantime turned Christian, so that, being a renegade, I deserved my countrymen's hatred worse than if I had been born one, but they all welcomed me, with frank cordiality commending me to God's protection. It is not fanaticism but the instinct of self-preservation that animates them when their cherished institutions are assailed by ignorant or unworthy representatives of Christianity.

Negroes are usually indifferent to any creed, and their conversion frequently depends on what substantial inducements the missionaries can offer. An English clergyman in Zanzibar once complained to me that the number of his flock varied with the state of the supplies sent out to him from home. Before the Negro can be embarked on a higher spiritual plane, he must have the religious instinct awakened in him. Here again, you must go slow!

In case I should be thought prejudiced on the score of unremunerated labour by blacks, I refer my readers to recent European testimony on the subject. Firstly, there are the communications of Reichhard to the German African Society, and secondly Mr. Joseph Thomson's book "To the Central African Lakes and Back"—both published in 1881. Let me conclude by quoting what an Englishman said to me, after I had left Zanzibar. He simply characterised the whole anti-slavery movement, with all its public meetings, as "humbug."

CHAPTER XVII

History of a Dynastic Plot

THE AUTHORESS LOSES HER MOTHER—FAMILY DIS-
SENSIONS—PRINCESS SALAMAH'S EQUIVOCAL
POSITION—SHE CASTS IN HER LOT WITH BAR-
GASH—WHO ASPIRES TO THE CROWN AND FORMS
A CONSPIRACY TO DETHRONE MAJID—BAR-
GASH'S HOUSE SURROUNDED—HIS ABDUCTION
IN WOMAN'S GARB—DEFEAT OF HIS PARTISANS
—HIS RETURN—AND REJECTION OF MAJID'S
PEACEFUL OVERTURES—THE PRETENDER'S
HOUSE FIRED ON BY BRITISH MARINES—SUB-
MISSION AND BANISHMENT OF BARGASH

SINCE my father's death I had lived at Bet il Tani
with my mother and Chole, happy in their love
and friendship. Then, after three years of my
complete felicity, an epidemic of cholera swept
the whole island of Zanzibar, carrying off several
people of our household every day. It was during
the hottest season that this epidemic broke out.
One night, unable to sleep in my bed owing to
the oppressive temperature, I ordered my maid
to spread a soft mat on the floor, hoping thus to
find coolness and rest.

Imagine my surprise, when, upon awaking, I
found my dearly beloved mother writhing in pain

at my feet. In answer to my alarmed enquiry about her state, she moaned that she had spent half the night there; feeling that the cholera would take her away, she wanted to be near me in her last moments. My dear mother's sufferings from the dread malady distracted me the more as I was unable to alleviate them. Two days she resisted, and then left me forever. My grief knew no bounds; I paid no heed to any warnings, but clung desperately to my mother's body, in spite of the danger of contagion. For I desired nothing more fervently than that God should call me to Him with the dear departed. The disease spared me however, and I bowed my heart in resignation to the All-merciful and All-wise.

At the age of fifteen I was now alone, fatherless and motherless, drifting like a ship without its rudder on the open sea. My mother had always guided me with prudence and good sense, and I suddenly stood confronted by the duties and responsibilities of an adult, having to care not for myself alone, but for my dependants too. Happily, the Lord has ordained that recognition of a duty is mostly accompanied by the strength to carry it out. So I was able to survey my position calmly, to arrange my affairs without calling in foreign assistance.

Yet new troubles lay ahead: almost involuntarily I found myself entangled in a plot against my noble brother Majid!

It looked as though, after my father's death, discord had come to reign among us forever. Difficult as the maintenance of perfect harmony between thirty-six brothers and sisters might have been under any circumstances, upon Seyyid Saïd's decease we divided into congenial groups of three or four. To strangers this situation was incomprehensible; even our closest acquaintances could not always make out the intricate factional system that prevailed. A loyal friend of my brother's, an intimate of my sister's, must forsooth become my bitterest foe, unless belonging to my particular circle. Though such a state of strife could have none but disastrous consequences, we were blinded by passion, and unreasonably pursued one another with hot hatred.

Personal intercourse soon ceased altogether. The numerous spies we all kept widened the gulf by reporting each word or move of an enemy. At night these worthies would appear for their reward, which varied according to the value or the venom of their news. Sometimes a hooded figure knocked at the porter's gate for admittance after midnight, and we were roused from sleep to interview the informer, who would depart lavishly compensated.

Majid and Chole were on the best of terms at that time, which pleased me greatly, since I loved them both from the bottom of my heart; they had treated me as if I had been their own child

NASIR BIN SAÏD

One of the royal family, visiting England with Bargash

after my mother's death. Yet the good feeling between them cooled by degrees on account of my brother Bargash, a complete rupture finally ensuing. Dearly as I was attached to Chole, I sorrowfully confess that she, not Majid, was at fault—although I cannot here detail the acts which led to the breach.

For myself this proved a period of inward struggles. Living with Chole, I took my meals with her, and during the day we were inseparable. When she began to avoid Majid, and to show animosity toward him in every way—quite without cause—I hoped I could remain neutral; indeed, I ventured to defend my innocent brother, whose only transgression lay in the point that he, instead of Bargash, was Sultan. Months and months I found myself 'twixt two fires, so to speak, hesitating which side to enlist on, and when the moment came that a decision brooked no further delay joined my sister Chole, who, though she was in the wrong, I yet seemed to cherish most, and whose ascendancy over me had grown absolute.

Majid, a thoroughly noble-minded man, had earned the love of his whole people; but he was ailing, and could not himself attend to all state affairs, consequently leaving many of these to his ministers. One of them, Soliman bin Ali, unfortunately possessed the knack of making himself indispensable. A cunning rogue, he gradually contrived to render his will supreme in the land;

the other ministers became mere ciphers. His arrogance prompted him to play master at every opportunity. Withal, he had not reached the years which Arabs respect, but was green as grass, and a licentious fop into the bargain. In his conceit and craft he sued for the hand of one of my stepmothers, mature enough to have been his own mother; he intended to get her large fortune into his clutches, and she was foolish enough to accept him—bitterly ruing it after the marriage.

So this evil spirit gained a commanding influence over Majid, at the same time surreptitiously fanning the flames of discord among the Sultan's brothers and sisters, the more firmly to establish his, Soliman's, power. Quarrel after quarrel occurred in our family, notables were neglected or slighted, and things came to such a pass that finally loud public murmurs were heard. It was a blessing that at least one faithful, competent minister remained, who to some extent counteracted Soliman's malignancy and his errors. But upon his other advisers Majid could not rely with certainty, which facilitated Bargash's course in fostering hostility to him among our relatives and the people. As Majid had but one daughter and no sons, Bargash came next in succession; that two elder brothers, Muhammad and Tueni, still survived counted for nothing: they lived in Oman, and Oman was a long way off. An Eastern heir-presumptive to a throne is always in haste to rule, without minutely considering the prior rights of someone else, and in the pursuit of his ambition too often throws scruples and fairness to the winds.

Thus Bargash. Frustrated in seizing the reins of government upon the death of his father, Seyyid Saïd, he had nevertheless clung to hope, and his plans appeared to take a propitious turn after he came into town, with his sister Meje from Bet il Mtoni. Their house lay opposite that occupied by Chole and myself. Scarcely had the pair across the street settled down, when a warm friendship sprung up between Chole and Bargash, who would sometimes spend the whole day with us. At this Meje took offence, which, being voiced in the presence of others, resulted in the two women becoming severely estranged. They ended by ignoring each other if they met, and peace vanished altogether from the two households. Glad though I felt to be no partisan concerning this new quarrel, the angry sisters yet drew me into it through sheer talking at me. My intimacy with two nieces of mine, Shembua and Farshu, brought them close to Bargash, so that they entered the league. They too lived opposite my house and Chole's, Bargash's residence being separated from theirs by a narrow lane.

Bargash's principal endeavour was to win over

as many notables and chiefs as he could. The Arabs are divided into countless tribes, of greater or lesser importance, each paying unconditioned obedience to its chief. Naturally, therefore, every prince strives to gain the adherence of one or more such chiefs—which he secures openly, or, by preference, in secret—that he may have some support to reckon upon in time of need. Promises of preferment of course play a great part in these negotiations. No tribe will ever desert its chief, so strong is loyalty and devotion among the Arabs. One able to write puts the name of his tribe under his own; my full signature includes the name Lebu Saïdi, the small but valiant tribe to which we belong. Entering into close relations, then, with several native chiefs, Bargash by degrees formed a sort of little court, and this started a scandal. Besides, the persons most frequently gathering at his house had bad reputations; they were a disorderly, turbulent crew. All decent people of course held aloof from his scheming and plotting. Still there were plenty of self-seekers, disappointed or vindictive, ready to help him, dozens of whom imagined themselves already promoted to high office, endowed with some other good place, or installed as comfortable beneficiaries—but all intent upon serving their own interests, not their patron's.

As these followers grew in number, the details of the projected rising took definite form. Majid,

in short, was to be seized, and Bargash proclaimed Sultan. At all hazards, an armed conflict
must be prepared for. Meeting after meeting
was held under Bargash's presidence in the night,
before the moon rose or after it went down.
Feverish excitement and universal mistrust prevailed. We perpetually believed ourselves
watched and spied upon; often we did the servants' work, so as to keep them away and ignorant
of our plans. We women stopped making visits,
and would rarely receive any. Bargash waxed
hotter, and more overtly demonstrative. He
began to neglect the Sultan's daily audiences,
ultimately refraining from attendance altogether.
This was looked upon—in consonance with Zanzibar traditions—as signifying a rebellious spirit,
and a subject ostentatiously so offending was liable
to punishment. No one could now but suspect
Bargash's hostility; in fact he himself commenced
to act with such recklessness, that the vigilance
of the royalists became thoroughly aroused and
his success in laying hands on Majid very
doubtful.

The Sultan made a final attempt to wean me
from my false notions before it should be too late.
Since, under the existing circumstances, he could
not visit me in person, and I had long shunned
his palace, he sent a favourite stepmother of mine
to plead with me. He begged me to desist from
plotting with his enemies, who were making a

tool of me, and from whom I might expect no reward; on the other hand, I might regret the consequences of persisting in my obduracy, for if there should be any firing my house could not be spared. But before my high-minded brother's warning arrived, I was already pledged to Chole and the pretender, and felt myself solemnly bound by the promise. My stepmother left me with tears running down her cheeks.

Although the youngest member of the conspiracy, on account of my being able to write I was made secretary-general, as it were, and did all the correspondence with the chiefs. Nevertheless I was old enough to feel pangs of conscience; I winced at having to order guns, powder, and shot for the destruction of innocent lives. Yet what could I do? Was I to break my word, and abandon my beloved sister in the hour of peril? Never! My devotion to Chole influenced me far more than any leaning toward her brother. He, the son of an Abyssinian, is a highly talented man, distancing all of us in perspicacity and shrewdness. Proud, overbearing, imperious, he was credited with a forcible character. How little he was liked is proved by the fact that of our whole family none but we four women and our twelve-year-old brother Abd il Aziz, Chole's ward, actually went over to his side.

Despite the vigilance with which our movements were watched, we continued as before, sometimes meeting under auspices extremely perilous. We fixed the day for an open revolt. Then, suddenly, Bargash's house was surrounded by troops. We of course expected the same fate, and that would have meant the death of every hope. Indeed, as afterward transpired, the ministers and some other officials had advocated a blockade of the three dwellings, to which Majid had refused his consent because he wanted us women spared.

Our plans had to be entirely changed. It was decided that all Bargash's partisans should assemble at the estate of Marseille, near the capital, where they should entrench themselves. This was no bad idea, since Marseille could easily be turned into a fortress, and could shelter several hundred men. Thence, accordingly, arms, ammunition and provisions were transported; the soldiers levied were quartered close by. From the new centre of agitation the cause would be propagated throughout the island. By straining every nerve we succeeded promptly; without a regular treasury for the expenses, we each contributed as we were able out of our private resources, not omitting to furnish a quantity of well-armed slaves.

Our work done of establishing Marseille as the conspiracy's new focus, we meditated a grand stroke. We concluded to abduct Bargash from his residence, so that he might escape to Marseille, and direct affairs from that place himself. Fully appreciating the terrible danger of the enterprise, we were equally undaunted in our resolution to carry it through.

On the memorable evening Chole and I left our house with a large retinue; in the street we were joined by our nieces with their servants, as prearranged. The whole company proceeded to Bargash's door. Here our van was stopped by the soldiers, these having no idea who was following. Upon being thus brought to a halt, I complained in a loud tone of the unwarrantable indignity, and peremptorily ordered the captain to be called for. This was an utter violation of custom and etiquette, but the issue justified anything, and the officer was dumfounded when Chole and I stepped out of the procession to accost him. We began arguing at him violently for allowing his command to interfere with us; speechless at first, he then muttered excuses, and finally gave way before our insistence upon visiting the prisoners. He even acceded to our request that we be granted a certain space of time.

Inside, we found both Meje and Bargash excited to the verge of distraction. They had peeped down from a window, and witnessed the dispute upon the result of which hinged success or ruination. A fresh difficulty arose, however, when Bargash, in his virile pride, objected to donning female garments, a juncture the more embarrassing as there was none too much time available. At last he allowed us to dress him up so that only his eyes were left visible, and little Abd il Aziz we attired similarly. Before starting we offered a prayer to the Omnipotent.

With Bargash between the tallest women, we quitted the house in leisurely fashion, chatting unconcernedly, though trembling the while lest the soldiers should suspect anything. But they made way for the procession with the deference due to our rank, and we went on unmolested. Once outside the town, Bargash and the boy got rid of their disguises, bade us a hasty farewell, and vanished in the direction of Marseille.

The rest of us returned home in small groups and by circuitous paths. It may readily be conceived that sleep was out of the question that night. Overcome by the frightful strain of the adventure, anticipating the morrow with terrified forebodings, and conscious that we had perhaps narrowly escaped death, we gave free vent to groans and tears, some fainting away from weakness. All night we imagined we heard the tramp of horses and the firing of muskets.

No later than seven o'clock came the disastrous tidings that our enemies were apprised of what had happened. The government could do nothing but meet the open rebellion by force, and therefore despatched several thousand troops, with artillery, to Marseille. That charming palace completely demolished, the outnumbered conspirators fled in disorder after a short, sharp engagement costing hundreds of innocent lives.

The reader will inquire how we women were punished for our daring participation in the revolt. We got no punishment whatever! Had not the decision rested with the high-souled Majid, surely we must have come off less well, our machinations deserving a severe penalty.

The next news was that Bargash, his men being routed, had come back to town, and entered his house by stealth. Of course everyone thought his intention was voluntary surrender to his brother. Majid, in fact, tried to make the expected act of submission easy for him. Instead of soldiers, he sent his nephew Suud bin Hilal, with the message that he would forgive and forget, upon Bargash's promise to renounce such doings for the future. Suud, a mild, benevolent individual, went alone on his embassy, to show how peacefully the Sultan was disposed. Bargash began by refusing him admission, demanding that the envoy—his senior by many years—should communicate the message from the street. Suud naturally declined, and after a long wait the door was opened just wide enough to let him in. He then found himself obliged to climb up, literally to climb up, the barricaded stairway. At the top he had to crawl through a trapdoor, after a heavy chest had been removed from it. Not content with forcing Majid's ambassador to enter in this humiliating

TARIA TOPON

An East Indian merchant who accompanied Bargash to England

manner, Bargash frustrated his mission by emphatically rejecting the Sultan's indulgent proposals.

Such obstinacy now left Majid no alternative but a second resort to violent measures, much as he shrunk from them. The English consul, with whom he conferred, persuaded him of the necessity of putting a final stop to these protracted disturbances, and offered his assistance to that end. A British gunboat, which happened to be lying in the harbour, was to heave to opposite Bargash's palace, land a party of marines, and, if this demonstration failed, begin a bombardment. In effect, the marines commenced by aiming a few rounds of rifle fire at Bargash's house, himself fleeing to its rear, with Meje and Abd il Aziz, for safety from the bullets whizzing about their ears.

At the first shot Chole burst into convulsive tears, cursing Majid and the government and the English one after the other, accusing them all in turn of wronging us outrageously. As the musketry firing waxed vigorous, the whole household went into a panic, for our residence was behind Bargash's, so that we were likewise exposed. Old and young, high and low, lost their wits. Some bade eternal farewells; some begged each other's pardon for past offences; the coolest began to pack up with a view to flight; others stood about wailing and lamenting, incapable of thought or action; others, again, set to praying, wherever they happened to be, in the corridors, on the stairs, in the courtyard, on the roof, which was protected by a palisade. The example of these last found followers, and by degrees the general agitation gave room to the calming assurance that not man's will but the Lord's must ever prevail, that human destinies are settled from the beginning of the world by the All-merciful and the All-wise. Thus did we all devoutly sink upon our knees, our foreheads next to the ground, betokening deepest humility and resignation in the face of God.

The peril increasing apace, Chole at last made our obstinate brother consent to submit. Contrary to every rule of propriety she ran to the English consul's in person, with this information and the request that hostilities might cease. At that time the Britons did not enjoy their present power in East Africa; they had as little voice in Zanzibar's domestic affairs as, let us say, the Turks in Germany's. Since 1875, only, have circumstances materially changed—thanks to England's slave policy—in her favour and in the direction of our people's total ruin.

Chole did not find the consul, but as the occupants of Bargash's house were just then exclaiming: "Peace, peace!" to the marines, the firing stopped, and a greater calamity was averted. Had the gunboat actually bombarded the pretender's palace, not he but a different Sultan would now be sitting on the throne of Zanzibar, and I should never have come to Europe.

To prevent like conspiracies from recurring, it was determined that Bargash be exiled to Bombay, and thither he was taken in a British warship, accompanied (voluntarily) by Abd il Aziz. This was done upon the English consul's advice. Probably the Britons wanted to keep Majid's heir presumptive in their own hands, with the object of training him nicely to suit their own schemes. Two years he lived in Bombay, when he returned quietly to Zanzibar, and finally, upon Majid's death in 1870, succeeded to the long coveted crown.

CHAPTER XVIII

A Term of Rural Residence

COMPLICATED RELATIONS WITH AN INVISIBLE
STEWARD—LIFE ON THE PLANTATION OF KIS-
IMBANI—AND OF BUBUBU—SALE OF BUBUBU—
IN TOWN AGAIN—RECONCILIATION WITH MAJID
—QUARREL WITH CHOLE—ORIENTAL HATRED
OF DISSEMBLANCE—GREAT FIDELITY IN FRIEND-
SHIP

OUR enterprise, begun with such high hopes, and
so thoroughly set at naught, had cost us dear.
Though my nieces were rich enough to take their
losses lightly, many of our finest slaves had fallen,
and others, invalided or mutilated, constantly
brought back to our memory the disaster we had
stirred up. But this was the least punishment
we could expect to reap from the evil we had sown.
Much worse was it for us—Chole, Meje, my two
nieces, and me—to be conspicuously avoided and
ignored by all of our rightminded relations and
friends, and simultaneously to feel that this
treatment was fully justified. Other people, who
disliked us, or hoped to curry favour with the
authorities by talebearing, took the greatest pains
to go on spying upon us. To ourselves this mat-
tered little, for our cause was now lost beyond

redemption; but the fact that we were still under suspicion, and being watched, kept away our few remaining friends, while even the crafty Banyans shunned us for a long time, eventually slinking in at night to praise up their Indian wares as impudently as ever. Our houses, once all a-flutter, like dovecotes, with people coming and going, were now oppressively lone and dreary, unfrequented by a single soul from the outside world. This situation becoming unendurable, I resolved to retire to one of my estates; my four erstwhile accomplices soon imitated my example, and left town to live in the country.

Since my mother's death I had rarely been to any of my three plantations, and then only for a couple of days at a time; after all my late vicissitudes, and all the discordant strife, I was therefore prepared to enjoy a term of rural residence doubly. I chose Kisimbani as the place distinguished by my dear mother's preference and by memories of her frequent visits there. But I also realised that I must take upon me the disadvantages besetting Arabian ladies who live alone, because of their enforced independence of male advisers.

The tyrannous etiquette of our country forbids us to speak even with our own functionaries if these be free men. Orders and accounts must then be transmitted through slaves, and as but few noblewomen understand writing few single ladies ever see a balance sheet from their stewards. If they provide the supplies for the household, and remit so much hard cash after the harvest, the mistress is usually quite satisfied. These revenues are produced by the disposal of cloves and cocoanuts; potatoes, yams, and other things coming out of the ground, we are too proud to sell, and the steward may do what he pleases with any of them not needed for our home consumption.

While I lived in town my steward Hassan came every week or fortnight to hand in his report, through one of my domestic slaves, and to ask for instructions, which I sent him through the same channel. To meet cases like this a room is reserved on the ground floor, where the men rest after their long ride on muleback, and refresh themselves with food and drink before returning home. Now, however, when I intended to stay at Kisimbani, Hassan became inconvenient; the poor fellow himself had to keep hiding and dodging lest he should accidentally see one of us women. I therefore transferred him to another plantation, appointing an Abyssinian—a slave, not a freeman —in his stead, who was intelligent (he knew how to read and write) and energetic. The Abyssinians in general are smart people, and we would buy them rather than Negroes when we had the choice.

So I could go about the estate to my heart's content, without fearing to embarrass my steward.

Photograph by Coutinho Brothers, Zanzibar

SUAHILI MOTHER AND CHILD

My domestic animals afforded me much pleasure; I spent several hours among them daily. I also enjoyed comforting the old and sick in their small, low huts, my servants taking dainties to them from my abundant table. The slaves' children—a sort of dividend accruing to the owner of the parents—I had sent to me each morning, to be washed at the well with *rassel*, and then fed. *Rassel* is made from the foliage of an Eastern tree, whose leaves, dried and powdered, produce a foamy substance through contact with water, thus resembling soap. Until their progenitors came back from the fields, at four in the afternoon, I kept them in the courtyard, where they played games under the eye of a trustworthy female serf. This was better for the little urchins than being carried about in the sun all day tied on their mothers' backs.

The free, untrammelled country life agreed with me thoroughly; I was delighted to have exchanged the tumults of the town for this charming rural place. Obedient to etiqeutte, the wives and daughters of the neighbouring notables called upon me, and soon I had guests in the house for weeks, even months, together. Strangers, too, sometimes came to rest in the men's room after a tiresome journey. This is an old custom with us. Kisimbani being situated at the junction of two busy roads, the number of these birds of passage was always considerable.

I maintained regular communication with the town. On alternate days two mounted slaves rode in, and brought me back the news. Two or three times a week, besides, I sent in a maid servant, who returned with messages from my friends and relations. The excitement supervening upon that woefully unfortunate conspiracy having abated, dissent nevertheless continued among my brothers and sisters—another reason why I was in no haste for renewed urban residence.

My happiness was complete but for one thing. I missed the sea—which I had been accustomed to gaze upon every day of my life. My three plantations all lay inland, but as I knew not what it was to have a wish unfulfilled, I decided to purchase one near the water. I therefore, after due negotiations, acquired the estate of Bububu. My domestic pets accompanied me thither, and no doubt were surprised, at issuing from their baskets and cages, to meet again in a new court-yard; apparently they relished the change as much as I did. I would sit watching them by the hour, or would idle along the shore, looking out upon the blue surface with the ships sailing down from the north toward the town and the swift fishermen's boats that glided by in quick succession.

At Bububu I was nearer the town, which was within easy reach by road or water. Here, in fact, I lived more sociably than at Kisimbani.

Three of my brothers came out frequently, either
on horseback or by boat, and we spent the time
happily together, chatting, eating and drinking,
playing cards, setting off fireworks. Not four
and twenty hours ever sped but one or two, though
sometimes no less than ten ladies would visit me,
whether for a short call, whether for several days.
My own sojourn at Bububu was, however, destined
to be exceedingly brief, deeply though I felt
attached to the place. Because Majid sent me
word that the new English consul had expressed
a wish to purchase Bububu for a country seat, and
despite my great unwillingness to part with that
cherished possession, I could not let the first
opportunity pass of showing repentance by making this sacrifice—toward one whom I had so
wickedly wronged.

About a week after I had left Bububu and
settled in town again, Chole came to see me one
evening. She was in a lively state of mind, as
I could not help noticing the very moment she
appeared. Indeed, she had come with the object
of upbraiding me for surrendering my estate to
the consul, and when I quietly remarked that this
was really my own business, she blazed out the
passionate accusation that I had sold my property
to gain favour with Majid, "the accursed," as
she called him. She then grew more violent still,
and at last tore out of the house with the excla-
mation: "You may choose between Bargash

and myself, and that Englishman's slave! Good-bye!"

From that day on I never saw Chole again, although I continued living in the town, and it was only after my departure from Zanzibar that she began to show a less hostile spirit. Meanwhile I had resolved to shun both Majid and Chaduji, so that the suspicion might not arise of Chole's impeachment having been correct after all. But there was a surprise in store for me.

A fortnight from the date of my arrival in town, who should come to me but Majid, escorted by a great retinue! He wanted to thank me, he said, for pulling him out of the dilemma with the English consul, to refuse whose request would have placed him in an unpleasant position. I muttered some incoherent phrases, and Majid went on to talk of other things, making no allusion whatever to the late conspiracy, thus generously allowing me to infer that he harboured no resentment on account of it. We parted the best of friends after he had asked me to return the visit to himself, Chaduji, and my aunt Assha, who was with them. But my performance of this simple act of civility was to cost me dear; to this day it is counted as a crime against me by the same people whom I aided in the plot to enthrone Bargash. Such jealousy may seem incomprehensible, yet was characteristic of our family when under the stress of factional contention.

The two parties existed as before, and intriguing went on unabated, though less overtly and less clamorously. The friction was the harder to endure as none concealed their opinions, but gave them unrestrained vent. For the Oriental is very candid by nature, and quite incapable of dissembling after the masterly fashion of the European. When he regards somebody as his bitter foe and opponent he rarely makes a secret of it, and cares not a jot if he grossly insults him by glance, word, or gesture. The fact is the Oriental does not understand how to behave in contradiction to his real feelings and beliefs; he is almost entirely ignorant of the formal politeness which people here adopt indiscriminately under all circumstances. The mere attempt to sham— difficult, anyhow, for our impetuous, hot blood —would invoke the aspersion of cowardice. Over and over again, in those days, I used to hear questions, like: Why should I show myself otherwise than I am ? Are not all my thoughts and feelings plain to the Lord? Why should I tremble or pretend in the face of man?

On the other hand, to see devoted and really self-sacrificing friendship, one must go to the East. Not as though such a relation were possible only there, but certain it is that if an Arab loves he clings to the object of his affection with a fidelity that moves mountains. Although class distinctions are nowhere more rigidly observed, nowhere do they count for less in a genuine friendship. Thus a prince treats a groom's son he is fond of just as he would a scion of noble lineage, and no differently; a princess will exhibit the same tenderness toward her steward's wife or daughter as to a lady of lofty rank. My sister Meje, for instance, took a girl of humble station to live in her palace, and her attachment to this poor and modest, yet clever girl, persisted until they were separated by death.

Sometimes an aristocratic lady will be a close friend to someone else's slave, not a Negress, to be sure, but a Circassian or Abyssinian. The slave is then very fortunate, because her patroness will buy her at any figure so as to set her free. This liberation is performed under legal auspices, establishing its inviolability. Should a man be thrown into prison, his best friend allows himself to be locked up in the same cell for a few hours every day. An exile his intimates will accompany. Mishap or sudden poverty means disposal over one's friends' purses; hence no appeal is ever needed for public contributions. We are accustomed to this from youth up; and look upon it as a matter of course.

CHAPTER XIX

ELOPEMENT FROM ZANZIBAR

ACQUAINTANCE WITH HERR RUETE—THE ESCAPE
—MARRIAGE AT ADEN—BRIEF HAPPINESS IN
HAMBURG—SUBSEQUENT GERMAN DAYS

DURING these dark days of dissension and strife
in our family, I was made happy by the attachment of a young German representing a Hamburg
commercial house in Zanzibar. Inexact reports
of the details connected with this event having
been published, I think it best to outline the story
in brief.

While my brother Majid reigned, Europeans
enjoyed great consideration. They were welcome
guests at his palace and his estates, and were
always the recipients of marked attention. My
sister Chole and I entertained pleasant relations
with the Europeans in Zanzibar, expressed by
the exchange of such courtesies as the country's
customs permitted. The European ladies in Zanzibar for the most part confined their visits to
Chole and myself. I made my future husband's
acquaintance after returning from Bububu. The
new house I then took was next to his, and his
flat roof a little lower than mine; from an upper

window I often witnessed the convivial men's parties which he gave in order to show me European meals. Our friendship, which ultimately grew into deep mutual love, was bruited about the town, and my brother Majid heard of it. His enmity toward me on this account, and my incarceration were, however, fictitious tales.

Naturally I wished to leave my country secretly, where our union would have been out of the question. The first attempt failed, but another opportunity presented itself. Through the mediation of my friend Mrs. S., wife to the English doctor and consular agent, I was one night fetched away in a boat by Mr. P., commander of the British war vessel *Highflyer*. No sooner was I on board than her engines began to move. The *Highflyer* took a northward course, landing me safely at my destination, the port of Aden. Here I was taken in by a Spanish couple, whom I had known at Zanzibar, and here I patiently waited for my intended. It took him a few months to wind up his affairs, when he followed me to Aden. Meanwhile I had been instructed in the Christian religion; my baptism—with the name of Emily —took place in the English chapel at Aden, being immediately succeeded by the marriage ceremony according to the Anglican rite. My husband and I then sailed for Hamburg, his native town, where his parents and other relations gave us a warm welcome.

"FREE CITY OF HAMBURG" BEFORE ITS INCORPORATION WITH THE
PRESENT GERMAN EMPIRE

From a contemporary local engraving

I soon got used to the foreign surroundings, and zealously learned all I could to fit me for my life here. My unforgetable husband watched the various stages of my new development with keen interest; he took a particular pleasure in observing the first impressions made upon me by European habits and customs. These impressions I recorded on paper, and may perhaps speak about in the future.

Yet our happy, contented existence was to last only a short while. A little over three years had elapsed from the date of our settling in Hamburg, when my dearly beloved husband chanced to meet with an accident in jumping from a tramcar. He was run over, and died after three days of intense suffering. I now stood alone in this great, strange country with three infants, of whom the youngest counted but three months. At first I though of returning to my home, but fate willed it that my own dreadful loss was followed, in two months, by the decease of my dear brother Majid, who had always treated me so kindly. He never even resented my secret escape from the island; as a true Moslem he believed in divine foreordination, and was convinced that this had determined my departure. He gave touching proof of his brotherly affection, not long before he died, by loading a ship with gifts, which were to be presented to me at Hamburg; none of the articles reached me, for, as I found out some years afterward, although the vessel came into port, Majid's intentions were dishonestly frustrated. I might add that he did not molest my betrothed after my sudden disappearance, but allowed him to transact his business in perfect freedom.

Two years more I stayed in Hamburg, constantly undergoing fresh misfortunes. I lost a considerable part of my property through the fault of others, and discovered that I had to take my affairs into my own hands. Complete aversion seized me toward the place where I had once known so much happiness, especially as among some people of the town I was not treated with that civility which was perhaps my due.

Removing to Dresden, I met with cordial friendliness in all circles. Thence I took a journey to London, of which the next chapter will tell. When, at a later date, I conceived the desire to live in a quiet town, I chose that delightful little capital Rudolstadt. There, too, I met with a great deal of genuine friendship and affection during the years of my residence, which their Serene Highnesses did their most to make agreeable. My health improving at Rudolstadt, I decided upon Berlin as a good place to educate my children. Once more I found many friends who tried to render my sojourn pleasant. Royalty itself manifested a gracious interest which I shall remember my whole life with sincere gratitude.

CHAPTER XX

A Piece of English Diplomacy

JOURNEY TO LONDON—INTERVIEW WITH SIR BARTLE
FRERE—THE CHOICE OFFERED—AVOIDANCE OF
MEETING BARGASH—RETURN TO GERMANY—
DISAPPOINTMENT—DUPLICITY OF THE BRITISH
GOVERNMENT—ITS MOTIVE

ALL this time I was in constant epistolary communication with home, which I never gave up the hope of visiting. But thus far my brother Bargash's obduracy had rendered any prospect of being made welcome by my family impossible. The reason for his persistent attitude of enmity was sheer vindictiveness: he could not forgive my having resumed amicable relations with his old antagonist, Majid. This did not, however, diminish my yearning for home and friends, and I went on secretly looking forward to a reconciliation.

In the spring of 1875 a report spread through the newspapers that profoundly agitated my whole being: my brother Bargash, Sultan of Zanzibar since Majid's death, was coming to London. At first I remained inactive, concealing my uneasiness, but I was prevailed upon—though after all my disappointments I had few illusions left—to bestir myself. So I concluded upon a journey to London, and Count Bülow, the German foreign secretary, led me to believe that I might expect diplomatic support from the imperial ambassador, Count Münster, which, alas, proved of little efficiency.

The short interval at my disposal I employed in learning English, so as to mitigate my helplessness. During those two months I would often pore over my books until dawn, conning words and phrases by rote. And then there was my growing anxiety about the three children, from whom I had never been separated for long.

Finally I started by way of Ostend. Worn out and nervous, I reached the giant metropolis, where my only acquaintances, Mr. and Mrs. P., kindly took me in, and did everything for me they could. Meanwhile, having arrived in London a week before Bargash, I called on Count Münster, who assured me of his good will. My friends in Germany had made me promise to act carefully, and above all to secure the English government's help in my cause. Originally I had felt disposed, as I had found out through experience how few people are to be trusted, to rely upon the Lord and my own efforts; but I yielded to my friends. The fear that I might be regaled with polite diplomatic formality and phraseology, and my affair then pigeon-holed, was a trifle compared to the actual course of events. For I had yet to learn that I was now in a world where lying and cheating counted almost as virtues.

EMPEROR WILLIAM I. OF GERMANY

One day Sir Bartle Frere was announced. This man, who subsequently became governor of the Cape Colony, I knew by name only, but if ever I put faith in a presentiment it was on that day, when my fondest hope and my children's future were both doomed. An indescribable feeling of uneasiness overcame me the moment I set eyes upon the great diplomat, who lorded it over Zanzibar at will, and had the Sultan in his pocket, so to speak.

The usual civilities exchanged, Sir Bartle began by inquiring into my affairs, and particularly wanted to know my reason for coming to London. Although he appeared to be perfectly informed already, I told him my exact object. There was in fact little to say, as I simply wished for reconciliation with my family. Imagine my surprise, therefore, when Sir Bartle coolly asked the question: Which was most important to me, this reconciliation or the security of my children's future prospects? Even now I scarcely feel equal to analysing the emotions aroused by his proposal. I had anticipated anything but a stroke of that sort. Let me be accused of cowardice or vacillation if I wavered at such a moment. The welfare of my children of course stood higher than my personal wishes.

On slightly recovering from the embarrassment into which this astonishing diplomatic manœuvre had thrown me, I requested that Sir Bartle explain the motive of his proposition. He then stated positively that the British government had no wish to mediate between myself and my brother, whom it regarded as its guest; and, whom, as such, it must spare any annoyance. (I am in doubt, nevertheless, as to what would have annoyed the Sultan most: signing the slave treaty under moral duress, and so indirectly acknowledging English supremacy, or holding out his hand to a penitent sister.) If I, on the other hand, would solemnly engage not to approach my brother, either in person or by letter, during his visit to London, the British authorities would guarantee the material welfare of my children.

Bitterly disillusioned, I now stood before the choice of acting independently and without English official assistance (but with the conviction that it would place insurmountable difficulties in the path of one too weak to overcome them), or of accepting governmental aid for my children. In view then, of the promise given to my German friends, not to go alone and unprotected to my brother—although I never thought he would offend against the laws of England even if I appeared before him suddenly—I assented to Sir Bartle Frere's offer. When, suspicious of the government's intentions, a friend of mine asked Sir Bartle how it had come by such a sudden benevolent interest in my case, that astute diplomat

COUNT BERNHARD ERNST VON BULOW
Foreign Secretary of the German Empire

returned no less than three reasons: 1st, We do the Sultan a favour; 2nd, We pacify the princess; 3rd, We anticipate the German Chancellor's (Prince Bismarck's) opportunity of taking a hand in this himself. All of which sounded plausible and reassuring.

To avoid meeting Bargash in public places, whether at museums or other buildings open to all, or in Hyde Park, or in the streets, I studied the newspapers, where his daily excursions were announced in advance. And I begged my amiable hostess to excuse me from driving out with her, but this she would not hear of because my health demanded that I take fresh air regularly. So, when the Sultan went east we drove west, and vice versa. This precaution I believed absolutely necessary, since I felt diffident about my strength of mind, and feared I might break my word if I actually did meet him. But it was not likely that in the European clothes I now wore even my sainted mother would have recognised me, much less a brother, who had usually seen me veiled.

I should have preferred to reëmbark for Germany, leaving behind me the place that had witnessed the defeat of my hopes. But even this satisfaction was denied me. Far from my children, I was to go on suffering untold agonies for weeks in a city where I had known nothing but grief and disappointment: Sir Bartle Frere had ordained that I must draw up a detailed memorial. Unversed in such matters, and mentally reduced to an automatic state, I gladly allowed my kind friends to undertake this report for me, supposing, naturally, that only good could come of it. When it was done, at the end of about six weeks, I went back to Germany and my children.

Zanzibar being then looked upon as a future British dependency, my memorial had first to be submitted to the authorities in India. A few months passed, until one day I received a letter from London. It inclosed the copy of a document which the British government had handed the German Ambassador for transmission to myself, and which contained nothing else than a brief rejection of that very memorial so urgently insisted upon by Sir Bartle Frere. As a reason for declining to consider the memorial, the document stated that I, having married a German, and living in Germany, my case would be of greater interest to the German government, This lame subterfuge was the more ridiculous as I had appealed for alms neither to the one government nor the other, but had solely asked for the moral support of both. Sir Bartle Frere had himself suggested the memorial—the same diplomat who had wormed out of me a vow to abstain from seeing my brother in exchange for my children's assured prosperity.

Whether such treatment of an unfortunate

SIR BARTLE FRERE

woman was worthy of a great country like England, I leave to the decision of the fair-minded. But I should like to ask if the British government, represented by Sir Bartle Frere, when it made that offer to me was ignorant of the fact that I had married a German, and was therefore a German subject? The point was never brought up when the promise was lured from me not to see my brother. I had kept to my part of the agreement faithfully and conscientiously. You perceive that while I was in a position to communicate with my brother, then I was not a German individual of no importance to the English, but the Sultan's sister, who might have harmed English interests; but lo and behold, after my brother had gone home again, I became innocuous, and this card was played to get rid of me forever.

Later on I was informed as to why the authorities wanted to prevent a reconciliation between me and Bargash. The Sultan being ignorant of any European language, and not understanding the refinements of European statecraft, the English were quite willing he should remain in darkness, for he would thus less likely balk when it came to signing certain treaties. If I made up with him, I, with some knowledge of European ideas, might tell him things advantageous perhaps for the ruler of Zanzibar to know, but inconvenient for the designs of the British government.

Yet I must note a great difference between the English government and English society, among which latter I encountered warm sympathy, and to some of whose members I shall feel indebted for the rest of my life.

CHAPTER XXI

Visit to the Old Home

EMBARKATION—ALEXANDRIA—EGYPTIAN DISLIKE
OF THE ENGLISH—TRAVEL IN THE SUEZ CANAL
—THE RED HOT SEA—ARRIVAL—WELCOME BY
THE POPULACE—CAUSING DISPLEASURE TO
SEYYID BARGASH—HIS OFFICIAL FACTOTUM
AN EX-LAMP CLEANER—DILAPIDATION AND DE-
CAY—BARGASH'S FRIGHTFUL CRUELTY—THE
AUTHORESS'S CLAIMS UNSETTLED—BRITISH IN-
FLUENCE OVER THE SULTAN—CONCLUSION

WHEN I penned the preceding chapter, a few
years back, I had almost entirely given up the
realisation of a wish that filled all my thought and
being. The eventful times since I had left my
Southern home had been a period of well-nigh
incredible stress and storm. I had gone through
the strangest experiences, including some that
one would not even desire for an enemy. By
means of a strong constitution I managed to
endure the severe Northern climate a long time,
but at last, yielding to my inclination for a change,
two years ago I conceived the idea of revisiting
Zanzibar with my three children.

Confidently I took the necessary steps, and
met with hearty coöperation from the authorities.

Matters dragged none the less, and I was about to despair anew of ever seeing my country again, when one day came a letter from the office of the imperial Foreign Secretary, bidding me hold myself in readiness for departure to Zanzibar. The news agitated me to such a degree that I did not immediately appreciate my good fortune. Next to praising and thanking the Lord for His wonderful guidance, I felt under profound obligations toward our revered, beloved emperor and his exalted government; my children and I shall always remember them with intense gratitude.

On the first of July, 1885, I started with my children from Berlin, safely reaching Trieste on the third, by way of Breslau and Vienna. Not until I was actually settled on board the Lloyd steamer *Venus*, which weighed anchor at noon that day, did I feel free enough from anxiety to enjoy the peace I had so sadly missed of late. The morning of the fifth we were at Corfu. A few hours' drive gave us acquaintance with the best sights of that charming island, whence we proceeded, past barren Ithaca, at Greece's southernmost extremity, and lofty Candia, to the port of Alexandria.

At setting foot on shore here, among the palm trees and the minarets, a warm sensation of homelikeness flooded over me, which can only be understood by such as have been long absentees under similar circumstances. The real South I had not laid eyes on for nineteen years; during this whole time I had sat by the stove in Germany, winter after winter. Even if I had become a Northern resident, with the multifarious duties of a German housewife falling to my lot, my thoughts were usually far, far away. I knew of no entertainment, no distraction that I preferred to poring over a book describing the South. No wonder if at the aspect of Alexandria I nearly went out of my senses, and stood watching the bustle of the harbour as if in a dream.

At the custom house we were required to identify ourselves. Resolved not to tell my name if it could possibly be avoided, I asked a travelling companion to lend me one of her visiting cards, which, to my astonishment, was accepted as sufficient proof. Literally besieged by the noisy mob, we had pains enough to get a cab, and so reach our hotel. Two dozen people surrounded us, clamorously offering their services, and persisting until driven off by the police. The cab could then begin to move, but not without one enterprising individual jumping on behind, and recommending himself loudly as an interpreter as we drove along; that I spoke Arabic myself, and therefore could do without one, seemed an incomprehensible mystery to him.

The two days we spent here at an hotel, which was dear and dirty, went by in a flash. I liked best going to the Arab quarter of the town, whose animated life afforded me continual pleasure. No sooner would I address the people in Arabic— they began by scanning me suspiciously—than their faces cleared, and their eyes lit up. "Mother," they would cry, "where did you learn to speak our language so well? You must have lived in Bagdad; how long were you there?" Our cabman took such a fancy to us that he finally besought me to take him as a servant; he swore he would be faithful to me all his life and would never touch a drop of my wine. The poor fellow was much grieved to learn that I could not entertain his project.

The once beautiful city of Alexandria still lies in ruins—a monument to English "humanitarianism!" Excepting the Viceroy of Egypt and a few of his ministers—mere creatures of Britain—all natives cordially detest the English. On several occasions I heard very disparaging remarks passed about them by people in the shops and the streets. I was repeatedly asked whether I was English, and when I said I was a German this would make a favourable impression. Neither has the European colony at Alexandria any better opinion of the English.

From Alexandria we got to Port Said in a passage of eighteen hours. Here we met the supply ship *Adler*, of the German East African squadron, and were taken on board. Although Port Said is but a small harbour town, you can

LADY FRERE RECEIVING SEYYID BARGASH AT A GARDEN PARTY

get almost anything there; the shops abound with all luxuries the heart of man could desire.

At this place begins the desert and the canal that runs through it, connecting the Mediterranean with the Red Sea. The channel is so narrow that vessels cannot pass each other. Species of sidings therefore exist at intervals, distinguished by signs erected on shore, as "Gare Limite Sud" or "Gare Limite Nord." A ship may have to wait at a siding for hours until one from the other direction shall have passed by. At Port Said every steamer takes on board a pilot, who knows how to get it safely through, understanding the ball signals run up on ropes which indicate whether you are to wait, how many ships you must allow to pass, and so forth. No ship may go through the canal at full steam, because a heavy swell might damage the unsubstantial sandy banks. Traffic is suspended altogether at night.

The channel widens at Suez, and we steamed through into the Red Sea. Oppressive enough in the canal, the heat became unendurable between the high rocky sides of the Gulf. We were bathed in perspiration day and night. As for me, the homelike temperature agreed with me capitally, but my children it did not suit, making them show irritation and enervation. The sea was running too high to permit the opening of the port holes, and as the air below grew thicker, we spent the night on deck in wicker chairs, uncomfortably and restlessly. The passage to Aden lasted a week, and there we stuck for five days before the *Adler* was ordered to continue on the voyage. On the second of August the isle of Pemba hove in sight, and, oh, what joy! For this meant that the coast of Zanzibar was no more than thirty miles distant, and easily attainable in three hours. But as night was upon us we stopped at the North Cape, since it would then have been dangerous to attempt the port, because of the sand-bars.

The following day we were up betimes. On the horizon the forest of masts in the harbour was visible. Steaming along the shore we could plainly discern the palm groves dotted with Negro villages. After much signalling an anchoring ground was assigned us, which we however had to change very soon. We found four German men-of-war lying in the harbour, the *Stosch*, *Gneisenau*, *Elisabeth*, and *Prinz Adalbert*, two vessels belonging to the English navy, five steamers of the Sultan's, and several sailing ships. Commodore Paschen thought it advisable to regard me as "secret cargo," a designation that greatly amused the officers of the squadron. But as soon as the gallant Admiral Knorr arrived with the *Bismarck* the situation altered, and I was free to go ashore as I liked.

Upon our first visit to the town I seemed to read unfeigned surprise in the countenances of the people who crowded about us. Right and left

SQUARE OF THE CONSULS, ALEXANDRIA

Result of bombardment by the British fleet under Admiral Seymour in 1882

they exclaimed, in Arabic and Suahili, "Welcome, mistress!" Did we enter a shop to make purchases, a vast throng would gather outside, respectfully making room when we emerged again. Day by day our voluntary escort grew in number, and the populace became more and more enthusiastic. This of course angered both the Sultan and his political adviser, the British consul-general; in fact Bargash had some whipped for following us. Then he and the English official saw fit to make a complaint to the commander of the squadron because of the popular demonstrations in my favour. Hearing of this, I warned the people against accompanying me any more, but they replied that the risk of punishment should not deter them. Slaves would approach me with messages from their mistresses begging me to accept the assurance of their fidelity and devotion; they wanted to visit me on board, and said their houses were open to me. Notes secreted under their caps were also surreptitiously slipped into my hand by slaves. Passing by a house I would sometimes observe ladies who had hidden behind the door in expectation; when I passed by they would speak to me, or would simply call out, "God be with you, and keep you in good health!" My brothers, sisters, other relations, and former friends repeatedly sent word asking me to come and see them; but I declined all these invitations, not from personal

reasons, but because compelled by circumstances.

If we went by the palace in rowboats, or under
the windows of the royal harem, the Sultan's
wives waved their hands to us; and as naval
officers accompanied us on our expeditions I was
obliged to request these gentlemen not to return
the salutes, for the ladies' own sakes. I even
avoided doing it myself, in order to save the
thoughtless fair ones from destruction, it having
been reported to me that their lord and master
was wont to hide somewhere in the palace, and
overlook the water or the street, so that he might
catch delinquents, and punish them. Nor is this
invention. It is quite well known that, a year
before my visit to Zanzibar, the concealed Sultan
detected a favourite—a lovely Circassian—exchanging salutations with a Portuguese who was
passing in a skiff. This is by no means a new
custom. I remember how, thirty years ago, in
the days of my childhood, we were bowed to by
Europeans, especially by French and English
naval officers, and by resident traders; we used to
acknowledge the compliment in the same way,
and never did our men folk raise the least objection.
Yet Bargash took a different view. He flogged his
Circassian so brutally with his own hands for the
offence, that a few days after she gave up the ghost.
He is said to have implored her forgiveness in vain;
he still has prayers said over her grave,

On our excursions into the interior we often met people riding on donkeys. To show their respect they would get off, lead the animals past by the reins, and then mount them again. Despite the Sultan's chastisements the inhabitants persisted in their demonstrations of attachment, and of course the shouts of "Kuaheri, bibi" (Farewell, mistress), resounding almost under his windows whenever we started back for shipboard, must have annoyed him. Every time our boats neared shore somebody beat an old biscuit tin like a drum—so I was told—to bring the people together.

Naturally there were always spies on our trail, mostly East Indians, to whose intense chagrin we conversed in German. The very evening before my departure, two faithful friends, who had ventured out to the ship under cover of darkness, called to my notice the sombre figure of a man who had frequently honoured us with his attentions as a peddler, the clever tool of the influential, quondam lamp cleaner and court barber, Pera Dauji. An excessively crafty Hindu, this individual has worked himself up to the position of a factotum to the Sultan, undertaking any kind of job, high or low. All diplomatic negotiations go through his hands, which same hands wait upon the Sultan's guests at table. He draws the huge salary of thirty dollars a month! Everybody in Zanzibar takes good care to keep on the right side of the omnipotent Pera Dauji, who, unable to maintain himself in such splendid raiment on thirty dollars, seeks other channels of revenue. The court jeweller, by refusing the ex-lamp cleaner a percentage on all of the Sultan's orders, lost this custom, which Pera Dauji transferred to a more pliable competitor.

Long residence abroad has perhaps made me fastidious; at any rate the inner part of the town looked to me in a deplorable condition. Ruins all along the streets, that were narrow and kept none too clean; ruins everywhere overgrown with weeds and even with trees sprouting up. No one seemed to care; everyone walked on indifferent, picking their way through a network of puddles and rubbish heaps. Ash and refuse pits are unknown—the open street serving their purpose. Nor can the art of municipal administration be quite easy, otherwise the Sultan, who has known the pleasure of clean streets in Bombay, England, and France, would have remedied the evil long ago, Meanwhile he has introduced the manufacture of ice, electric light, a so-called railway, and other fine things, not least of them French cooks and cookery.

The terrible decay of the inner town was most painful to me, but as yet I had no notion in what state I should find my venerable Bet il Mtoni again. Coming upon the place where I had first beheld the light of day, I sustained a severe shock. What a spectacle it was! Instead of a house an

COMMERCIAL STREET, PORT SAID

utter ruin; not a sound to rouse me from the depressing sensation caused by the unexpected sight. It took me some time to recover. One staircase was completely gone, the other overgrown and shaky enough to be dangerous. More than half the house was in ruins, left just as it had fallen; the roofs had vanished from the bathhouses, some of which were represented by piles of rubbish; the parts still standing were likewise floorless or roofless. Dilapidation and decay at every hand! In the courtyard all manner of weeds flourished. Nothing was left to remind the spectator of the former splendours of that palace.

Having alluded in this final chapter to the head of our family in Zanzibar, I feel tempted to unveil a few more episodes from his career. It cuts me deeply to expose one of my own blood, for, all the years of separation from my people notwithstanding, and regardless of Bargash's cruelty toward me, who once staked life and property for his success, I have yet an inextinguishable sentiment of family affection. But Seyyid Bargash is a man without a grain of compassion either for his subjects or his closest of kin.

It is commonly known in Zanzibar how, upon succeeding to the throne, he imprisoned his next brother, Khalifa, *sans* reason or excuse. For years the unfortunate languished in iron footrings weighted with chains. Why? Nobody ever could tell. Perhaps he feared that Khalifa, being nearest in succession, might head just such a conspiracy as himself once had fomented against Majid. When a sister whom he had affronted was starting on a pilgrimage to Mecca, Bargash's conscience disturbed him, and he entreated her pardon; he dared not face a curse invoked upon him in the Prophet's holy city. Yet she declined to forgive him until he released his innocent brother.

Nevertheless, Bargash continued to keep an eye on Khalifa and his friends. Learning that one of his brother's intimates was well blessed with worldly goods, he recollected how alliances with rich chiefs had once been important to himself, and determined to rid his heir presumptive of any such valuable support. So he sent for Khalifa's friend, and said to him, in substance: "I have heard that you propose to sell your plantations; tell me how much you expect, as I should like to acquire them." "That must be a mistake," replied the other; "I never had an idea of selling my property." "But," returned the Sultan, "it will be to your advantage if you sell me your land. Think the matter over."

Soon he was summoned into the royal presence again, and once more he explained that he had no design of selling, this time however receiving the conclusive answer: "It is not of the slightest consequence what your intentions may be. I will give you fifty thousand dollars. Here is an

order for the money." Sorrowfully the poor
wretch took himself off—to meet with a still worse
blow. Because when he tried to cash the order
he was informed that the sum was payable in
twenty yearly instalments of two thousand five
hundred dollars each. The man was therefore
ruined—exactly what the Sultan had planned.

Another incident, that makes me blush with
shame, and fills my soul with pity: A malicious
piece of slander had spread concerning one of my
sisters; she was alleged to be in love with someone
not approved of by Bargash for a brother-in-law.
The Sultan went to her, charging her with the
offence. In vain did she protest total ignorance
of the affair: this tender-hearted brother personally administered fifty lashes to his own sister
with a cane! As a consequence she was laid up
in bed for a month, and suffered from the effects
of his brutal treatment long after. No doubt he
will some day have prayers said over her grave, as
in the case of his Circassian wife.

You often hear how highly Europeans praise
the Sultan of Zanzibar's affability; the real truth
may be judged from what I have written about
him. Certainly, at the bottom of his heart he
hates nothing more than the mere name of a
European. And what of his pretended friendship
toward Germany? I fancy the German East
African society possesses material enough to dis-
prove it.

That I could not expect much from Seyyid
Bargash in liquidation of my private claims may
readily be understood. The newspapers spread
the fictitious report that I went back to Germany
in full possession of my inheritance, this amounting
to the proceeds derived from the sale of twenty-
eight houses. I received not a single penny; my
claims, acknowledged as just even by the British
consul-general—and that is saying a great deal—
remain unsettled to this day. The stupendous
figure of six thousand rupees (about five hundred
pounds sterling), which my opulent brother proffered as a total settlement, I declined with thanks.
Since Bargash's accession five of my brothers, five
sisters, my aunt Assha, three nieces, one nephew,
and a rich stepmother have died, and I am entitled
to a share of all their property. The Sultan rejected the reconciliation with me suggested by the
German government in empty phrases; he must
have congratulated himself when my personal
affairs became overshadowed by political questions.

Another unpleasant matter. Everyone familiar
with Zanzibar is fully aware that the Sultan rules
but in small things, whereas the British consul-
general manages the rest. His very enemies admit
him to be an accomplished diplomat. Now, were
I as inexperienced as to diplomatic practice and
strategy as I was ten years ago, and did I take
each well-sounding word for true coinage, I should
most likely have believed what the consul-general

THE PORT OF ADEN

told a high officer belonging to the German fleet
—that he regretted immensely not to have been
able to do something for me—that unluckily no
opportunity had presented itself for him to see the
Sultan and to express my wishes in that quarter.
I soon discovered that a fortnight earlier the gentleman had spent several days with the Sultan
on one of his estates. One also hears of an active
telephone wire connecting the Sultan's palace with
his Britannic Majesty's consulate-general.

While nearing Zanzibar, I felt extreme doubts
as to the reception that awaited me there. I
hardly expected my brother would disregard
German wishes entirely, and I was not mistaken.
And I was prepared for his merely tolerating my
presence in the island out of consideration for
Germany. The villainous treatment he had given
other brothers and sisters of mine certainly prog-
nosticated no friendly spirit. But then there
was the further question—how would the people
take my arrival? To which I can fortunately
answer that I got the warmest welcome. Arabs,
Hindus, and natives all joined in begging me to
spend the rest of my days in Zanzibar. This con-
firmed my belief that they entertained no religious
prejudice against me for having turned Christian.
Indeed, one Arab said that he always looked upon
me as my father's daughter, that my change of
religion had been decreed from the beginning of
the world, that my departure and return had both

been ordained under the Divine will. "And now,"
he added, "surely you and your children are going
to stay with us."

Such proofs of attachment and devotion, combined with the blissful joy of having seen my dear
country once more, have sustained my soul in
many a heavy hour, have made my voyage an
event of lifelong happiness, and I cannot but
humbly offer repeated praise and gratitude to
God for His great goodness and mercy.

My second parting from home was not accomplished without bitter pangs, shared by my friends,
of whose farewell letter, written in Arabic and
sent to me in Germany, I now give a literal transla-
tion as a fitting conclusion to my book:

"They went hence without telling me they were
going;
   That tore my heart, and filled my soul with a
consuming fire.
   Oh, that I had clung hard to their necks when
they left us:
   For they might have sat on my head and
walked on my eyes!
   They dwell in my heart, and when they went
   They hurt my soul as it had never been hurt
before.
   My body is wasted, and my tears flow without
ceasing;

One after another they roll over my cheeks like the waves of the sea.

Oh, Lord of the universe, bring us together ere we die,

Even though it be but a few days before!

If we live, we shall meet again,

And when we die the immortal part of us shall survive.

Oh, that I were a bird:

Then would I longingly soar away after them!

But how can a bird fly whose wings are clipped?''

THE END

www.ingramcontent.com/pod-product-compliance
Lightning Source LLC
Chambersburg PA
CBHW070735270326
41927CB00010B/1996